GW00986224

TEXTILES IN BALI

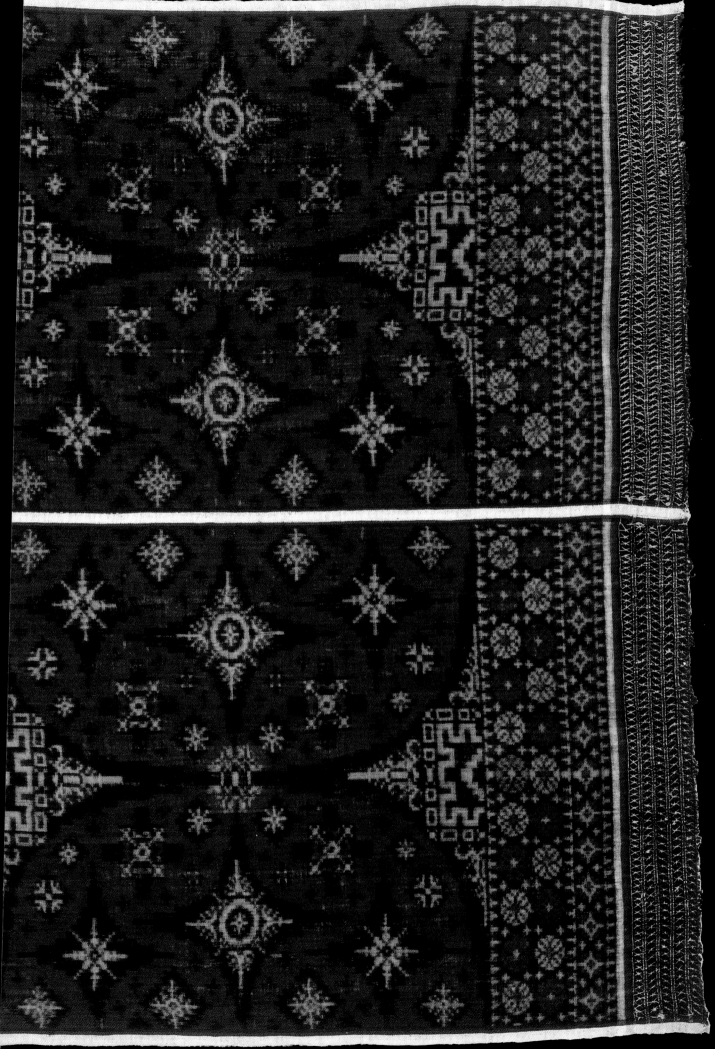

TEXTILES IN BALI

by Brigitta Hauser-Schäublin,
Marie-Louise Nabholz-Kartaschoff
& Urs Ramseyer

PERIPLUS
EDITIONS
BERKELEY-SINGAPORE

Published by Periplus Editions, Inc.

ISBN 0-945971-29-X

© 1991 Periplus Editions, Inc. and the Basel Museum of Ethnography

Title of German edition: Textilien in Bali

Publisher: Eric M. Oey
Design and Production: Peter Ivey
English Translation: Dennis Q. Stephenson
Photographers:

B. Hauser-Schäublin—*figures 1.1, 1.5, 1.7, 1.10, 1.11, 1.12, 1.13, 1.14, 1.15; 2.5, 2.6; 3.10; 7.2, 7.3, 7.4, 7.5, 7.6, 7.7, 7.8, 7.9, 7.10, 7.11, 7.12, 7.13*

Rio Helmi—*pages iv, x-xi, xii-xiii*   U. Ramseyer—*figures 3.7, 3.12; 5.10; 8.14*

Peter Horner—*jacket, pages ii-iii, ix; figures 1.2, 1.3, 1.8; 2.1, 2.2, 2.3, 2.4, 2.7, 2.11, 2.12; 3.1, 3.2, 3.3, 3.4, 3.8, 3.14, 3.15; 4.1, 4.2, 4.4; 5.1, 5.2, 5.5, 5.8, 5.9; 6.1; 7.1; 8.1, 8.4, 8.5, 8.11, 8.12, 8.15, 8.16; 9.1, 9.2, 9.3, 9.4, 9.5, 9.6, 9.7, 9.8, 9.9, 9.10, 9.11, 9.12, 9.13, 9.14, 9.15*

M.L. Nabholz-Kartaschoff—*figures 1.4, 1.6, 1.9; 2.8, 2.9, 2.10, 2.13; 3.5, 3.6, 3.13; 4.3; 6.2, 6.3, 6.4, 6.5; 7.14; 8.2, 8.3, 8.6, 8.7, 8.8, 8.9, 8.10, 8.13*

Barni Palm—*figures 5.3, 5.4a-c, 5.6, 5.7, 5.11, 5.12, 5.13, 5.14*

Illustrations:

B. Hauser-Schäublin—*figures 2.14, 2.15*   S. Gisin—*figures 3.9, 3.11*

Captions to Photographs:

Pages ii-iii: *Geringsing lubèng*. Tenganan Pegeringsingan, presumably early 20th century. 168 x 119 cm., made by joining two widths of weaving. MEB IIc 18003.

Page iv: An old woman carrying sacred paraphernalia draped in *geringsing* at a temple ceremony. Karangasem, Asak.

Page ix: Outer hip cloth for men (*kampuh*). Colored rayon and gold threads on silk. Presumably Tabanan, 1920-30. 162 x 112 cm. MEB IIc 20294.

Pages x-xi: A procession of several Barong, Rangda and other sacred masked figures at a temple ceremony. Presumably North Tabanan.

Pages xii-xiii: A Barong Landung couple and other gods at a *melasti* purification ritual. Gianyar, Singapadu.

Distributors:

Indonesia: C.V. Java Books, P.O. Box 55 JKCP, Jakarta 10510

Singapore and Malaysia: Periplus (Singapore) Pte. Ltd.
P.O. Box 115, Farrer Road, Singapore 9128

Hong Kong: China Guides Distribution Services Ltd.
14 Ground Floor, Lower Kai Yuen Lane, North Point

Thailand: White Lotus Co. Ltd., GPO Box 1141, Bangkok

The Netherlands: Nilsson & Lamm bv, Postbus 195, 1380 AD Weesp

United Kingdom: British Museum Press
46 Bloomsbury Street, London WC1B 3QQ

United States of America: University of Washington Press
P.O. Box 50096, Seattle, WA 98145-5096

Printed in the Republic of Singapore

Contents

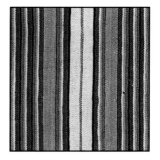

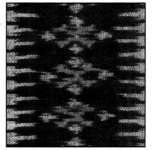

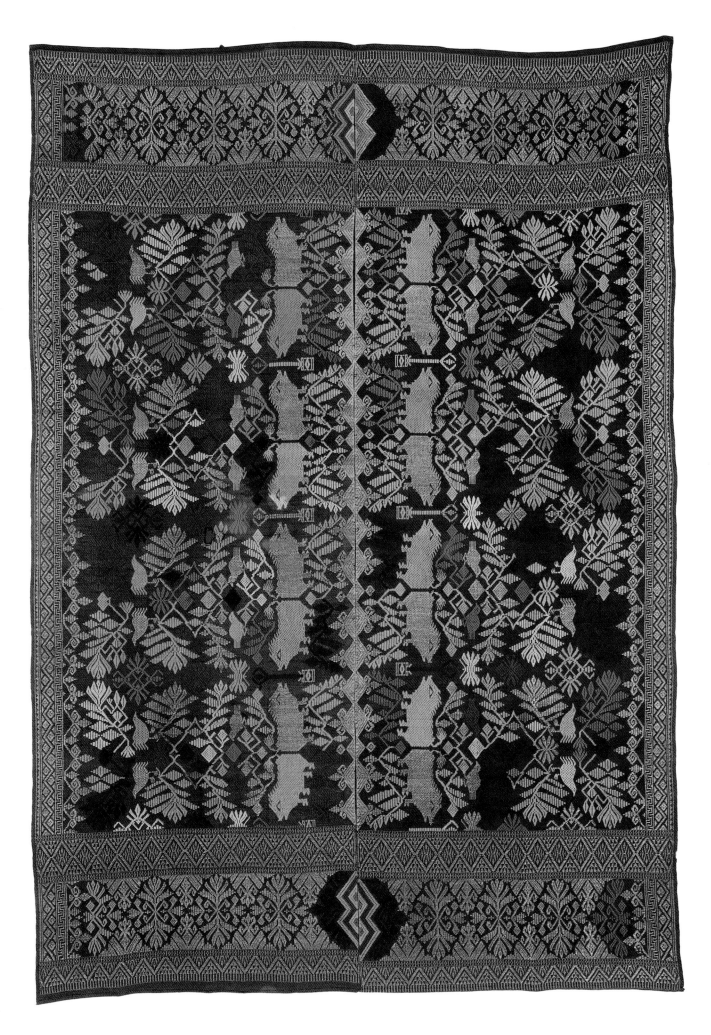

Preface

The title of this book succinctly intimates what it is all about—textiles in Bali. It is concerned pre-eminently with the manufacture, use and significance of various textiles which reflect the island's great cultural richness and diversity. We have never ceased to be fascinated by the way in which tangible objects here—namely cloths and textiles of every kind—can become infused with a life of their own. Nor have we ceased to be intrigued by a manner of handling such textiles which, while using their materiality as a medium, never makes it an end in itself. Nevertheless this book has material origins, without which it would never have come into being, namely the renowned collection of Balinese textiles in the Basel Museum of Ethnography, where two of the three authors are curators.

The genesis of this collection goes back to the years immediately preceding and following the Second World War, but there are certain pieces which date from the turn of the century. The criteria observed in its composition are not antiquity, (Western) aesthetics or sumptuous quality. Rather, since it is a collection based on scientific principles, importance has been attached primarily to obtaining a broad variety of examples of the textile craft, with reference to the materials and techniques employed as well as to their regional origins and to their functions and meanings.

For these collections we are indebted primarily to the Basel ethnologist Paul Wirz (1892-1955), the ethnologist and textile specialist Alfred Bühler (1900-1981), and the painter Theo Meier (1908-1982). This "Bali tradition" has continued to flourish at the Museum of Ethnography and the University of Basel down to today. The present volume is a testimony to this.

We have documented these textiles during several visits to the island, and have done so in terms of "textiles in Bali." Urs Ramseyer made a study of *geringsing* cloths such as are produced only in Tenganan, most of his work being done in 1972-74. All other textiles presented in this book were documented by the three authors between 1988 and 1990.

The book is divided into chapters according to the most important categories of textiles, although these admittedly make up only a cross-section—albeit a representative one—of what is actually a far richer textile life in Bali.

If, as previously mentioned, the collection of the Basel Museum of Ethnography forms the material basis for this book, it does so more especially in the sense that it was the starting point for intensive research. The book represents an initial summing up of this documentary work. It shows how textiles are embedded in the cultural matrix of Bali, and tells by whom and under what conditions textiles are made as well as when, where and how such cloths are used. It shows clearly how the weaving techniques, patterns, dyes and materials used form the "raw material" from which is spun a fine network of cultural significations and interrelated contexts of meaning. Our attempt is to direct the reader's attention from the material to the non-material—to the social and the semiotic. In other words, textiles are presented here as a cultural "language," to the understanding and interpretation of which we have addressed our special attention.

Many of the textiles are works of art in their own right. However, we have refrained from a contemplation of their aesthetics since this would inevitably involve alien, non-Balinese criteria. It is therefore left to the reader—if he will—to proceed to an aesthetic assessment of the textiles; no hierarchy of values is proposed.

Precisely because of the importance of textiles in Bali, expecially in rituals of all kinds, the book was written not only for textile devotees and readers interested in Bali but also for the people of Bali itself. There is no other reference work covering the wealth of their textiles. Moreover, the indigenous textile handicrafts of this island find themselves coming under severe pressure from new and differently—mainly commercially—oriented values, as it has become a holiday paradise for visitors from faraway. The upshot is that the diversity of traditional textiles has begun to diminish and a great deal has already fallen into oblivion. At the same time, however, the textile crafts have received a new impetus and—with the creativity characteristic of Bali—have struck out along novel lines, with astonishing and compelling results.

The documentary work underlying the book has been rendered possible by two factors: support by institutions in Switzerland (Swiss National Fund, Department of Education and Culture of the Canton of Basel City, Voluntary Academic Association) and in Indonesia which made possible our journey and stay, and the people of Bali who met us with never-failing cordiality, allowed us to share their life, and answered all our questions with great patience.

Our gratitude to our friends in Belayu, Beratan, Intaran and Sanur, Kerambitan, Kusamba, Legian, Sidemen, Tenganan and in Nusa Penida is more than we can express with this book.

—*B. Hauser-Schäublin*
—*M.L. Nabholz-Kartaschoff*

Sanur, November 1990

CHAPTER ONE

The Universe Arrayed

Textiles in Bali

FOR anyone coming from a distant country, landing at Bali's Ngurah Rai International Airport is a memorable experience. He is lapped in warm tropical air, to his ears come the first snatches of the Balinese language, and when he expectantly steps outside the airport building, a colorful picture meets his eyes: taxi drivers and travel agents are dressed in dark trousers and light-colored shirts, while younger people mill about in blue jeans and brightly emblazoned T-shirts. Smartly dressed hostesses from major hotels and tour companies have come to welcome the new arrivals and conduct them safely to their temporary residences.

The journey from the airport to any other destination leads past a statue of I Gusti Ngurah Rai, a Balinese hero in the national struggle for freedom and independence. The crowded highway leads past shrimp nurseries bordering the coast, while cattle graze in fields by the roadside. Men, women and children travel on foot, astride bicycles or motorbikes, and in cars and minivans. Some of the children sport blue-and-white or red-and-white national school uniforms, while adults are dressed in the international style now common the world over. Overall, the impression is one of a prosperous, thriving island.

Just as one is beginning to think, however, that Bali has succumbed to the dictates of international fashion, an unexpected sight meets the eye. In the midst of the streaming traffic is a family riding on a motorbike: the father, who is driving, is not wearing long trousers but a batik hip cloth covered by a somewhat shorter yellow cloth with a gold-and-white border. His white shirt flutters in the wind, while around his head is tied a cloth—a standard element of men's festive apparel. Perched on the gas tank, between his father's legs, is a four-year-old lad, also in traditional dress: a *songkèt* hip cloth matching his size, a white T-shirt and, like his father, a headcloth. The mother sits side-saddle behind her husband. Her long wraparound is of *endek* material in various shades of blue, with a *kebaya* blouse in a matching solid color. A broad sash of the same *endek* material is wound around her waist over the blouse and hip cloth, setting off her slender figure. Her face is made up with care, and her long black hair is tied in a bun that drapes down gracefully at the back of her head. In her hair are golden flowers that nod and wave with every movement.

Figure 1.1 (opposite): For an annual temple festival the central shrine, representing a holy mountain, is decorated all over: a universe arrayed. Sanur.

Figure 1.2: First attempts at weaving on the *cagcag* loom. Karangasem, Sidemen.

Figure 1.3 (opposite): Hip cloth. Cotton and *bagu* yarn. Supplementary weft and *endek*. Batur region. 214 x 108 cm. MEB IIc 15969.

On her lap the woman holds a silvery metal offering dish with a splendid tower of artistically-arranged fruits and brightly-colored Balinese cakes. Obviously the family is on its way to a temple festival to present their offerings to the gods, to pray and to receive their blessings in return. Cycling circumspectly along the roadside is a man dressed in white from his headcloth to his skirt: he is a *pemangku*, a temple priest, on his way to perform his daily ministrations in his sanctuary.

On arrival at one of the major hotels, the visitor is greeted by Balinese employees wearing outfits modeled after traditional clothing. The apparel is tasteful in color, flattering the figures of men and women alike, imparting sensuous grace. This contrasts sharply with the holiday garb of Western visitors who, regardless of their physical stature, seem to insist on wearing the scantiest possible clothing wherever they go. While this may be tolerable at the beach, at a temple festival such disregard for propriety is a serious insult to the Balinese and to their gods!

Visitors to the major towns who browse in shops and admire the range of goods on display—from antique carvings to ultramodern computers— are bound to come across many fashionable textile products. Boutiques have on display clothes made from materials with patterns and designs that are replaced every few months by new ones. Designers, dyers and seamstresses in many small to medium-sized clothing firms churn out a bewildering array of inexpensive garments for the fast-moving international trade, partly to fill orders received from the industrialized countries. Though such fashion products lack nothing in inventiveness or creativity, they are by no means "traditional" or "Balinese," and there is only a tenuous link between these fabrics and the traditional crafts of

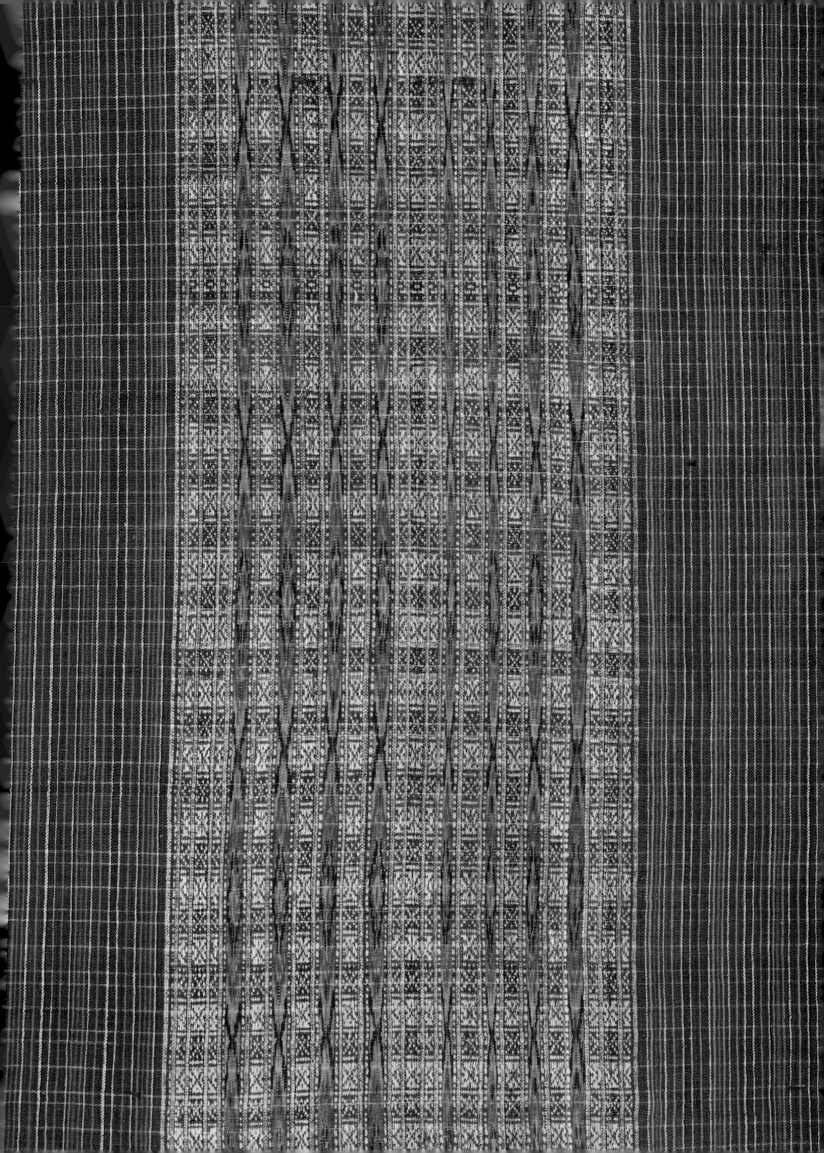

cloth making. Just as culture and people are changing in response to the opening up of the island by tourists, so the products intended for these visitors are constantly being adjusted to meet the new needs and demands they create.

ORIGINS

Bali has a long history, the greater part of which is obscured by the mists of time, and archaeologists have only just begun to bring to light small fragments of this past. Written records begin in the 8th century A.D., and the story told in these early inscriptions and chronicles mirrors the influence of the great Javanese empires. Their courts were attended by Buddhist and Hindu scholars—literati who partly were instrumental in propagating these religions of Indian provenance. A sustained change thus took place in the culture and society of Bali, in which mercantile influences from China, India and other islands of the archipelago also played a role.

In discussing the traditional textiles of Bali—in describing the complicated techniques used to make double *ikat geringsing* (see Chapter 9), the patterning of *cepuk* (see Chapter 8) and *perada* (see Chapter 4)—it quickly becomes apparent that their origin must be considered to a great extent against this historical background. It would be wrong, however, to attempt to explain these textiles and their uses in terms of a single origin or a single line of development. The great diversity of Balinese textile arts—their independence, creativity and rich traditions—points to a long and continuous evolution within the context of the island itself and its culture. Thus textiles of the most diverse kinds have quite specific

Figure 1.5 (above left): Temple festival after renovation of the sanctuary. Rich variety of textile adornments and offerings. Sanur.

Figure 1.6 (above right): A textile stall's colorful display at a market in Denpasar.

Figure 1.4 (opposite): A procession on the occasion of a great purification ceremony for the souls of the dead. Sanur.

functions and meanings which are typical of Bali, and cannot be understood on any basis other than that of Balinese culture itself.

According to written tradition (the *Purana Bali* text), the inhabitants of the island were originally ignorant of rice cultivation in terraced and irrigated fields, of metalworking, and of the growing and use of cotton. They formerly went about virtually naked, says the same source, although they did make loosely fitting garments of bark cloth, fashioning loincloths by passing long strips of pounded bast fibers between their legs and around their hips.

Though to the best of our knowledge there are no bark cloth garments from Bali to be found in any museum collections, memory of the material and its use lives on, especially in remote mountain regions. During the difficult times of the Second World War, sleeveless open jackets of bark cloth were revived in mountain villages. In addition to this bark cloth, it is said that a thread from the leaves of the *bagu* plant (Boehmeria nivea Gand, white ramie) was spun and woven into fabric (Fig. 1.3).

The *Purana Bali* also states that it was the goddess Ratih, wife of the god Semara, the Raja of the Invisible, who, together with her companions, instructed mankind in the cultivation of two types of cotton—transcribed in Indonesian as *kapas cicih* and *kapas tahun*. Rocky soils and (non-irrigated) *ladang* fields were well suited to these crops. The goddess taught the entire process of working the cotton to make finished cloths for men and for women. She also supplied the necessary equipment—the traditional *cagcag* loom (Fig. 3.11) on which to make *songkèt* and *endek* materials. In addition, she taught them elaborate techniques of dyeing.

The percipient observer, refusing to be misled by stories of a *tabula rasa* in Bali created by Hinduism and Buddhism of a Javanese and more recently Chinese cast, will no doubt discern many archaic elements in Bali. Textiles are no exception. Apart from the bark cloths already mentioned, such elements include a large number of plaitings and braidings. Plaited mats still figure importantly, however in a way that is visually unspectacular and is therefore commonly overlooked. They are indispensable in shrines, where they are used as underlays for offerings and figures of gods. They are also used in death rites to wrap the mortal remains of the deceased before cremation. Hangings of light beige and rich green strips of young palm leaves, known as *lamak*, appear prominently and are likely to catch the eye of even the casual observer. These are most commonly rectangular in shape, and are used for the ritual adornment of offering stelae and shrine niches. They are also hung like bibs around the necks of "cremation bulls" before the latter are borne to the cremation ground (Fig. 1.15). There are many sizes of palm-leaf *lamak* with different patterns, sometimes with additional red ornamentation. Although the matter has not been investigated in detail, it is reasonable to assume that *lamak* patterns and sizes are specific to the particular locality and occasion. In other words, different types of *lamak* are used depending on the place, the festival and the deity being worshipped.

In addition to such rapidly perishable plaitings, there are also more durable textile *lamak* (Fig. 1.8) whose patterns are sometimes identical with those made of palm leaf. These are treasured as heirlooms and carefully preserved, and are brought out solely for the important annual

Figure 1.8: *Lamak,* ceremonial hanging for abodes of the gods. Supplementary warp on cotton. Bali, near Denpasar. Pre-1940. 176 x 52 cm. MEB IIc 15946.

Figure 1.7 (opposite): Textile *lamak* serving to adorn an abode of the gods in a stone temple. South Bali.

temple festivals, where they are attached to the abodes of the gods (Fig. 1.7). Today the most common form of *lamak* has a hard base trimmed with Chinese *képéng* coins and mirrors. These are suspended from shrine niches, while beneath them another palm-leaf *lamak*, invisible to the observer, serves as an underlay.

Another element that appears to be of archaic origin is the short sleeveless jacket worn today by the main ritual protagonists in a particular temple festival near Denpasar (Fig. 1.13). Although these jackets look as if they were tailored exclusively from red, green or black material (sometimes trimmed with gold ornamentation), they resemble similar garments that are made from bark cloth in what are known as "Old Indonesian" cultures—as among the Toraja in South Sulawesi and also on the islands of Sumatra and Nias. But here again the material is of a special type. Concealed under the colored cloth is a layer of coir fiber which gives the clothing a special significance. According to informants, these jackets fall into the category of martial and battle garments, and were sometimes lined with leather instead of coir for protection. Those on the lookout for persistence in textile forms and materials will continually meet with such survivals from the past and evidence of local and regional cultural traditions.

TEXTILES AS SEMIOTIC SIGNS

Figure 1.9 (above left): Tower of textile offerings for a wedding. Nusa Penida.

Figure 1.10 (above right): Stone with *polèng* waist cloth. P. Kutri, Buruan.

In Bali, textiles are much more than just cloths from which garments are made. Beginning with the yarn itself (*benang*) and the woven textiles, they are a medium through which the divine nature of the universe and its material manifestations are recognized and expressed. The inner spirit

of the world—both the natural world and that created by man—expresses reverence and adoration for its creation. It is a world view that does not place individual man at its hub, or subordinate its environment to him, but rather one in which the divine nature of the living world occupies the center. This view is expressed in the places and ways in which textiles are used. One often sees, for example, enormous broad-crowned trees around whose trunks a white or black-and-white checked cloth is bound; while below it there are flowers, both fresh and faded, and petals from sacrificial offerings. One may also see upended stones of a curious shape which have been draped with a cloth like a wraparound (Fig. 1.10).

These everyday testimonies to an omnipresent divinity appear during ceremonies and annual temple festivals in an even more pronounced and immediate form. The members of a procession accompanying the divine figures and symbols to the strains of the gong orchestra are each adorned and arrayed in festive apparel; the procession itself is led by banner carriers whose flags and pennants—textiles secured to poles—announce from afar the extraordinary significance of such a procession. Over the floral symbols of gods and the carved anthropomorphic and zoomorphic figures of deities clad in specific textiles (Fig. 1.11) is a textile firmament of ceremonial parasols (Figs. 1.15 and 7.5).

It is also quite common to witness processions, especially to and from a Brahman house compound, in which the women form a long line, each carrying a white cloth of the same length over her head. Cloths are also spread out on the ground to maintain the ritual purity of those stepping over it and to prevent them from direct contact with the soil, which

Figure 1.11: Zoomorphic figures of gods are dressed for a temple festival. Sanur.

Figure 1.12 (above): A sanctuary is invested with an aura for an annual festival: shrines and halls are draped with textiles. Sanur.

Figure 1.13 (top right): At certain temple festivals the *pemangku* ritually dress in sacred fabrics. Their form and materials (coir fiber trimmed with red, black or green fabric) are handed down from the past. South Bali.

Figure 1.14 (above right): Holy water vessels wrapped round with colored yarn. Colors correspond to the cardinal directions. Pura Leluhur, Uluwatu.

represents the chthonic or earthly (as opposed to the uranian or heavenly) principle (Fig. 7.14).

The customary appearance of Balinese temple sanctuaries, with their offering stelae, shrines and open pavilions, is gray, forlorn and lonely. For the annual festival when the deities are invited to descend, however, these sites are transformed. The individual abodes of the gods, the shrines and the pavilions, are all made ready for the arrival of the gods and are dressed on the same principle as the human body (Fig. 1.12). Two wraparounds, one representing the upper hip cloth and one the cloth beneath, are draped around the pillar on which a small shrine stands; both are secured with a sash. Above the offering niche, the structure is adorned with a headband modeled after a man's headcloth. The niches themselves, at least in south Bali, are lined with plaited mats, with a *lamak* hanging down. The walls of the pavilions for offerings are draped with textile hangings, and the places for the divine figures and for the brahman priest (*pedanda*) are adorned additionally with a white canopy (white being the symbol of ritual purity). Among the offerings presented to the gods are carefully folded cloths used solely for this purpose, usually placed on offering dishes next to the divine figures. In Nusa Penida such cloths are sometimes piled into high "offering towers" (Fig. 1.9). Sacrificial animals are also clad in cloth, and even the wooden cremation bull which serves as a sarcophagus for the those of high social status is fitted with an integument of fine white cloth which transforms it into a divine escort for the soul of the deceased (Fig. 1.15).

It is the textile itself, the woven object, that betokens divinity—but colors, material and pattern more precisely define its character. In this

connection we might mention the rose of the winds and the gods and colors correlated with it in Balinese cosmology (cf. p. 60). One can tell from the color used for, say, the veiled abode of a god, what type of deity must be involved. Red cloths are used for an altar to Brahma (god of fire and blacksmiths; his cardinal direction is south), whereas black cloths betoken Wisnu, and so forth. The same is true of the cloths tied on the backs of sacrificial animals; their color indicates the gods to which they are dedicated. Offerings placed in small earthenware dishes are also arranged on the principle of the cardinal directions, with their particular gods and meanings, this being indicated by the dyed yarns with which the holy water vessels are wrapped (Fig. 1.14).

Today preference is shown for certain colors: white and yellow, which symbolize the divine generally (Fig. 1.4). The combination of various colors in the same cloth, and the way in which they are combined, may signify ambivalence, danger and, at the same time, protection and defense (see Chapters 7, 8 and 9)—for gods and their attendants are not only celestially pure and benevolent, but may also be dark, dangerous and minatory.

Finally, certain categories of textiles supply information relating not only to the gods, but to the social aspects of humans, their characteristics and the relations between them. For the individual, cloths of a special kind such as *bebali* and *wangsul* (see Chapter 5), mark various stages of human life and are used to protect the individual in ceremonies of transition. Certain textiles formerly expressed the highly stratified social hierarchy of traditional Bali. Such materials as *bebali* and *wangsul* were produced and controlled by the *gria* or brahmanical houses, while at the

Figure 1.15: "Cremation bull," draped in white cloth, gold paper adornments and palm-leaf *lamak*, accompanied by two ceremonial parasols. Amlapura.

CHAPTER TWO

Endek

Ikat Production in Transition

THE form of traditional textile most commonly seen on Bali today is *endek*. This is the most highly-developed process in terms of technique and design; largely as a result the fabrics have acquired many new, non-traditional uses and are now seen far beyond the island's shores. Once the prerogative of noble families, *endek* has become a popular article of dress and an important badge of cultural identity for Balinese men and women of all social classes.

The patterning technique known here as *endek* is actually a variant of the *ikat* process widely practiced throughout Indonesia. *Ikat* (Indonesian "bundle," *mengikat* "to tie") is a complicated and time-consuming resist-dye technique in which undyed yarns are mounted on a frame in bundles according to the pattern and tied in places with short lengths of banana bast or plastic strips. During the dyeing process, the tied areas resist the absorption of dye and remain uncolored; repeated tyings and dyeings can result in a multihued pattern of great intricacy. The preprogrammed designs may be applied to either the warp threads alone (warp *ikat*), or to the weft (weft *ikat*)—or to both thread systems at once, so that the patterning of each one supplements the other (double *ikat*).

Two forms of *ikat* are known in Bali: weft *ikat*, called here *endek*, has the pattern in the weft only; double *ikat*, known as *geringsing*, has patterns in both the warp and the weft. The latter procedure is exceedingly complicated, as the two designs have to be brought precisely into register with one another, and is undertaken in only one place in the whole of Indonesia—the tiny village of Tenganan Pegeringsingan in eastern Bali (see Chapter 9). In recent years, combined warp and weft *ikat* processes have been used in some establishments in Gianyar (central Bali) as well, but here the warp is patterned in some places and the weft in others, while the two are never blended together as in Tenganan.

COURTLY SYMBOLS OF STATUS

For a long time *endek* cloths were solely the prerogative of the princely families of Bali. They were worn on special occasions in palaces and temples as sumptuous wraparounds (*wastra, kampuh*), as breast cloths (*seléndang, anteng*) or as shawls (*cerik*), frequently containing added *songkèt* or supplementary weft patterns (see Chapter 3). Elaborate production methods and exotic imported materials such as silk, special dyes, gold

Figure 2.1 (opposite and above): Outer hip cloth for men (*kampuh*). *Endek* and *songkèt* on silk. Bulèlèng, 1920-30. 141 x 109 cm. MEB IIc 17571.

and silver threads greatly enhanced the value of these traditional status symbols of the courtly culture.

The earliest extant *endek* textiles date from the late 19th to early 20th centuries and come from the north Balinese principality of Bulèlèng, which was at this time an important and influential textile-producing center. *Endek* patterns from this period are predominantly geometric, and are combined with *songkèt* patterns to form an artistically unified whole. *Endek* crossbands patterned with lozenges, crosses and arrowheads alternate with strips of geometrically patterned *songkèt*. Likewise, *endek* triangles with small, multicolored dashes nest together with contrasting *songkèt* ones to form rectangles. The basic color of these early *endek-songkèt* fabrics is red—varying from a deep purple-red to a warm brick-red. Only later do yellows and greens appear.

Early figural representations are rare and very sumptuous, consisting for example of *patola* patterns with lions and riders on elephants (see Chapter 8). This tendency to imitate patterns produced by other techniques—thereby creating, as it were, a substitute product—can also be observed in *endek* versions of the *geringsing patelikur* double-*ikat* cloths. The dominant feature of these *geringsing* cloths, highly esteemed throughout the island for their ritual and magical properties, is the large four-pointed star with crenelated internal pattern which divides up the surface of the fabric into large, semicircular segments (see Chapter 9). Outside Tenganan this pattern is known as *kota mesir* (from *kota*, etymologically meaning "battlements," in modern Indonesian and Balinese "town;" and *mesir*, "Egyptian," often referring to swastikas and other meander-like patterns). At the beginning of our century, it came to be applied to silk *endek* fabrics from Bulèlèng; in the 1930s it was imitated in Nusa Penida (possibly also in Lombok) in coarse materials of handspun cotton with dark backgrounds. Recently this pattern has cropped up again in mercerized cotton cloth sold by the meter (from Sidemen and Sampalan, near Klungkung), and has now gained acceptance as the *dernier cri* for wraparounds worn by Balinese on festive occasions (Fig. 2.13).

At the beginning of the 20th century, *endek* cloths from Bulèlèng came to be produced without the addition of *songkèt* in small strips of fabric which women wore as breast or shoulder cloths, and in broad outer hip cloths composed of two widths of fabric sewn together. Here again some of the patterns, such as tiny, flowering trees, are reminiscent of the *patola* motifs (Fig. 2.2, left). Innumerable *endek* silks containing geometric *cepuk* patterns with their characteristic rows of *gigi barong* ("*barong* teeth"—see Chapter 8) also date from this period. Other designs create a more expansive effect, forming huge flowers and stars (Fig. 2.7). One of these stylized four-petal patterns (Fig. 2.2, right) has survived to the present day and is still woven in one of the *puri* or palaces of Singaraja in Bulèlèng under the name of *tampak bela* ("poinsettia blossom").

Figure 2.2: Breast or shoulder cloths (*anteng, cerik*). *Endek* on silk. Bulèlèng, Bubunan, first half 20th century. 294 x 46 cm.; 252 x 41 cm. MEB IIc 17574; 13992.

During this period, the range of figural *endek* patterns was greatly extended. Depictions of the evil witch Rangda with flaming hair and lolling
tongue, as well as of the demon Kalarau (who according to Balinese
belief swallows the moon during eclipses) and many other gods and
demons—even the much-beloved "go-between" or *penasar* figures from
the Balinese *wayang* play (Fig. 2.4)—became popular motifs in *endek*
cloths of exceptional artistic merit. The placement of these figures at
right angles to the direction of the woven piece—technically a very difficult feat—is required by the way the cloths are worn as garments. Their
production is said not to have been confined to Bulèlèng at this time,
and the princely courts of Karangasem and Klungkung in eastern Bali
are also believed to have been centers of *endek* weaving. In this period,
the *puri* of Tabanan and Kerambitan also produced a unique geometrically patterned *endek* with multicolored stripes known as *serapit*. Uncer-
tainty still prevails as to the precise origin of certain coarse, gauze-like
endek fabrics with similar geometric patterning that were used as ceremonial cloths in Gianyar and Tabanan (Fig. 2.3). Their patterns and their
names, recorded by foreign observers already in the 1930s, suggest a
certain affinity with *cepuk* cloths (see Chapter 8). Like the latter, they
were used as ceremonial textiles in rites of passage and as decorations
at the courts.

AN OLD TECHNIQUE WITH NEW POTENTIAL

During the 1930s, the tradition of *endek* production and use began to
detach itself from the closed world of the courts and underwent a re-
newal. In many villages in Tabanan, and even on Nusa Penida, weavers
began to make simple *endek* materials from handspun local cottons or
from factory-produced and patterned yarns on traditional *cagcag* looms.
At this time a dyehouse in Denpasar began marketing factory-patterned
endek yarns in large quantities. New techniques and new designs
appeared employing loud colors on cotton, silk and soon afterwards on

Figure 2.3: Ritual cloth. *Endek* on
gauze-like cotton. South Bali, first half
of 20th century. 71 x 43 cm.
MEB IIc 14014.

Figure 2.4 (following pages): Overskirt
(*kampuh*) with depictions of Wisnu (on
horseback), Garuda, Naga and Twalen.
Endek and *songkèt* on silk. Karangasem
or Klungkung, first half of 20th century.
154 x 114 cm. MEB IIc 7514.

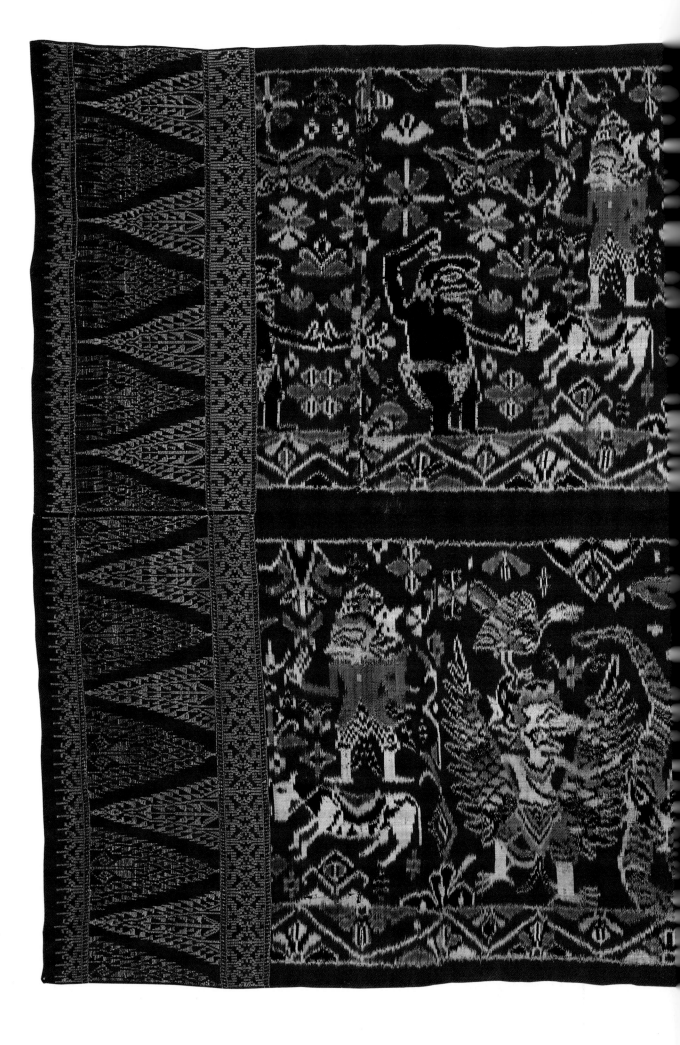

rayon, and new segments of the population became potential customers and wearers of the fabrics as a result. What proved to be the decisive factor, besides the abundance of new geometric and floral motifs, was that the production was no longer completely limited to individual cloths in specific sizes with a surrounding border, but consisted to some extent of yard goods with a continuous pattern for sale by the meter.

After independence, this development proceeded at an explosive rate. During the 1950s, the first large workshops were set up in Gianyar and these have now grown into important manufactories. In the 1970s, workshops large and small mushroomed all over Bali—in Sidemen, in the Singaraja area, in Sampalan near Klungkung, and in the neighborhood of Negara (Jembrana, west Bali). By 1989-90 there were 160 commercial *endek* producers in Bali employing a total of 10,042 people, and the production of checked, striped, plain and *endek* materials from cotton as well as man-made fibers and silk had by this time burgeoned to an average of 188,000 meters per month.

The profusion of new patterns reflects the astonishing creativity and technical skills of the Balinese. The modern *endek* style has changed, and is now dominated by small repetitive geometric designs suitable for traditional and modern dress as well as for furnishings and decorative fabrics. Some workshops also look to the past and copy patterns from old Balinese and east Indonesian originals, while in Lombok one factory has even commissioned a famous American designer to create new patterns.

At the same time, the *endek* dyeing and weaving techniques have undergone thorough changes—indeed, far more thorough than those of any other Balinese textile tradition. This process of modernization has been marked by such decisive innovations as the application of new and more efficient winding and warping methods, the use of more convenient tying materials, the introduction of fast-acting synthetic dyestuffs, and a changeover from the traditional *cagcag* or backstrap loom to the new ATBM loom. A brief look at the individual production stages and a comparison of older methods with newer ones will clearly show how radical these changes have been.

Figure 2.5: Dyeing of *endek* bundles. Karangasem, Sidemen.

The first step in the *endek* process is the winding of threads and their separation into bundles corresponding to the pattern, so that tyings may be applied. The threads are drawn from bobbins suspended on a rack, and wound on a revolving frame that is the width of the cloth to be woven. The weft threads for four meters of cloth were formerly drawn from four bobbins; today the yarns are drawn from racks with 24 to 32 bobbins, yielding cloth lengths of up to 15 meters.

The tying technique has remained basically unchanged, although now rubber strips or flat plastic string are used instead of vegetable banana bast, as they are easier to apply and make a considerably better resist. Different colors of plastic make it easier to visualize the overall design. Familiar patterns can be reproduced from memory, while complicated and novel motifs are achieved using auxiliary lines drawn from sooted threads and/or a finished cloth or a drawing.

Improved bobbin wheels (Fig. 2.8) and large warping winders have resulted in great economies of labor. Traditional warping equipment such as is commonly used in *songkèt* home weaving was once employed (see Chapter 3, Figs. 3.9, 3.10), but the length of the warp produced by such means was limited. Today warps of up to a hundred meters in length are prepared on large winders that are driven by electricity in the more modern establishments.

The use of synthetic dyes in place of traditional vegetable dyes commenced very early and resulted in major changes in both technique and form. In 1908, Dutch administrators in Bulèlèng bemoaned the loss of quality in *endek* materials dyed with gaudy aniline dyes. Today naphthol or indanthrene and helanthrene dyes of Indonesian, Japanese or East European manufacture are used to the exclusion of all others (Fig. 2.5). The range of shades has been extended, and the dyeing process has been simplified and shortened. Whereas at one time some tyings were removed and new ones were applied for each new dye bath, today only a single bath is used to dye the basic color. The resists are then removed and the bundles arranged, stretched and hung up; other colors are then applied directly to the threads with a pair of toothed bamboo sticks, and

Figure 2.6: Partial dyeing of *endek* yarn. Karangasem, Sidemen.

rubbed in (Fig. 2.6). This simplified method of application (*nyatri*) became established in the 1930s and is possible only with synthetic dyestuffs. The winding-off devices for separating, winding up and spooling the colored weft yarns on bobbins have also been modernized.

The last and most crucial technical development came with the introduction of faster looms. In 1928, the first experiments were made with treadle looms set up in a few small workshops in Denpasar and Klungkung. During the Second World War, the Japanese introduced a modernized treadle loom on which coarse cotton cloth and sugar bags of coconut fiber yarn had to be woven. This so-called ATBM loom (*alat tenun bukan mesin*, or "unmechanized loom") was adapted to the needs of *endek* weaving during the following decades, and its use has been widely promoted by government programs and loans. Today it is used in all major workshops and manufactories (Figs. 2.9, 2.10).

The ATBM is a treadle loom with four pedals, a suspended batten, and two shafts with metal heddles for tabby weaving. Its most important feature, however, is a rapid-throwing mechanism which moves the shuttle to and fro automatically on the backward motion of the batten. On the ATBM, as much as two meters of material can be woven per day. The traditional *cagcag* loom is still used for weaving *endek* in less modernized areas, or by women who still weave a combination of *endek* and *songkèt*, as the complicated *songkèt* patterns cannot be produced on the ATBM.

CONDITIONS OF PRODUCTION

Endek textiles, usually in the form of finished clothing, are seen today all over the world—either as souvenirs brought home from Bali, or as commercial products on the international market—and it is natural to wonder about the conditions under which the fabrics are made. All *endek* cloths are still handwoven, and are therefore especially appreciated in industrialized countries where people must usually do with machine-made goods. "Handwoven" means that the cloths have either been made on a handloom at home or in a manufactory by a woman (less often by a man) weaver. Buyers who are not quality-minded often allow themselves to be dazzled by the low prices of cheap, imitation *endek* prints from Java and Lombok, not realizing the enormous amount of work that goes into the carefully tied bundles of yarn and the dyed patterning of genuine handwoven *endek* fabrics.

Developments of the past several years have established a clear pattern: only the larger manufacturers are able to adjust rapidly to changing dictates of fashion and demands of the market, while selling their products at competitive prices. Competition is fierce, and only establishments

Figure 2.8 (top): Winding of weft yarns with a modern bobbin wheel using a bicycle wheel. Karangasem, Sidemen.

Figure 2.9 (center): Weaving room in an *endek* manufactory. Karangasem, Sidemen.

Figure 2.10 (bottom): Weaving *endek* on an ATBM loom. Karangasem, Sidemen.

Figure 2.7 (opposite): Overskirt (*kampuh*). *Endek* on silk. Bulèlèng, first half of the 20th century. 160 x 106 cm. MEB IIc 19971.

with a keen, market-oriented management and first-class production methods have a chance of survival. Individual weavers who try to market their own products can no longer keep up.

Manufactories vary in size. In the village of Sidemen they have anywhere from 5 to 30 ATBM looms (Fig. 2.9); those in Gianyar have even more. The looms are set up in rows in a large hall and run from early morning—usually just before daybreak—until evening. Goods for sale by the meter are woven on ATBM looms, yielding bales measuring about 80 meters in length. A skillful weaver can produce up to two meters of *endek* per day.

Some manufactories loan single looms out to women with several small children so they can work at home. Materials, colors and patterns are determined by the manufacturer—usually a family-run operation—and given to the women with appropriate instructions. Thus the homeworkers produce directly for the manufactories, the only difference being that their workplace is at home. The quantity produced by homeworkers, because of the double job they have to do, is noticeably less than that of women in the manufactories, most of whom work an 8-hour day (sometimes longer, as they are paid according to output).

DIFFERENT TYPES OF HOME-WORK

There are significant differences between women who produce *songkèt* at home and those who produce *endek*. Women from all levels of society weave *songkèt* at home, not always out of direct economic needs but sometimes to earn a bit of extra money. Their economic position is thus strong—they become money-earners through their weaving and sometimes defray the greater part of the costs of maintaining a family. *Songkèt* weavers work on *cagcag* looms which are their personal property; they select their own yarns, colors and patterns themselves and buy what they need to weave cloths which appeal to them and of which they are proud. They sell to dealers or take the textiles to market themselves. They much prefer not to become dependent on contractors who are an encroachment on their autonomy. If money becomes short, they may always solicit orders for execution with borrowed material and predetermined patterns.

Endek home weaving, on the other hand, is not encountered among households from every social class. Only families with no other means of income will try to borrow a bulky ATBM loom to enable the women to earn money by weaving at home. Since the homeworker receives the loom and the material on loan, she is highly dependent on her employer. Precisely because she cannot concentrate on her work for any length of time without being disturbed, her quality is often below that of cloths produced in the manufactory. At the same time, depending on her domestic commitments, she is far less dependable when it comes to meeting delivery dates. Factors that can be clearly calculated and foreseen in the manufactory are often much vaguer in the home. These pressures often impose suffering on the home weaver.

A SIDEMEN MANUFACTORY

Let us consider two examples more closely, taking a manufactory first. The entrepreneur, a man of initiative who is receptive to new ideas, has

Figure 2.11 (preceding pages): Half of an outer hip cloth for men (*kampuh*) with a depiction of the demon Kalarau. *Endèk* and *perada* on silk. Karangasem or Klungkung, 1920-30. 143 x 68 cm. MEB IIc 18513a.

Figure 2.13 (above): Women attending the cremation of a brahman priestess, dressed in formal apparel with a wraparound skirt of *songkèt* and *endek* in the *geringsing* style.

Figure 2.12 (opposite): *Seléndang. Endek* on silk. Bulèlèng, early 20th century. 292 x 48 cm. MEB IIc 17573.

Figure 2.14: A weaving manufactory in a compound. **1**) Sanctuary with abodes of the gods; **2**) Open reception area for customers/employees; **3**) Dwelling house; **4**) Production hall (19.5 x 8 m.); **5**) Storage sheds; **6**) Kitchen/ bath; **7**) Experimental corner for new patterns; **8**) Veranda with workplace for entrepreneur's wife; **9**) Sales shop; **10**) Fountain with small garden; **11**) Drying frame for dyed yarn.

ATBM loom

Small ATBM loom

Workplace for tyer and stick dyer

Bobbin wheel

Warping device

House post

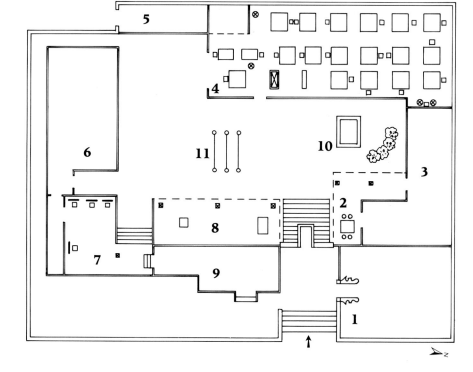

set up a production unit in the precincts of his house compound. He bought the land and built on it with the aid of a bank loan in the 1970s. The layout (Fig. 2.14) has characteristic Balinese features: it is enclosed by a wall with an entrance gate affording access to the lower compound. The sanctuary is located in the northeast—a direction considered particularly pure and divine. Opposite it, to the southwest, are the kitchen and bathroom. This direction is regarded as ritually more "polluted" and is set aside for physical needs. The dwelling and sleeping quarters are also built on the preferred northern side.

The manufactory sits in the northwest corner. There as many as 26 people, mainly women, weave, prepare warp and weft, and reel. The southeastern corner is for experiments; there men are busy tying and dyeing bundles of yarn to develop novel patterns. The sales shop is on the southern side, facing the street. In the inner courtyard is a fountain (the compound is, however, supplied with running water), a small flower and herb garden, and a drying frame for the dyed strands of yarn. The actual dyehouse is about 100 meters away from the compound and is annexed to the house of the entrepreneur's second wife. There, two people are engaged in dyeing the warp and the tied sets of weft threads (Fig. 2.5); as many as nine young men are busy dabbing on the additional dyes (Fig. 2.6). The workers, male and female, all come from the lower social classes and are between 14 and 26 years of age. Some have been there since the business began; they started at the age of 15 or 16 and still hold the same jobs today. The looms are operated almost exclusively by women (Fig. 2.10). Men work on the warping and reeling devices (Fig. 2.8) and all the dyers and tyers are also men.

Of the 33 men and women on the payroll of the manufactory, three are from a neighboring village and three from Gianyar. In earlier years, when the owner was starting up, he brought over a number of women *endek* weavers from Gianyar who were already experienced in using ATBM looms. But now there are enough women from the village who, with a knowledge of *songkèt* weaving on the *cagcag* loom, have been

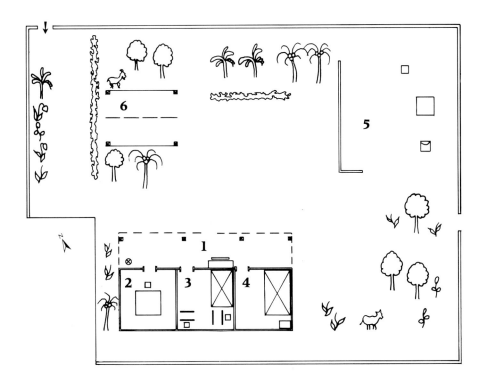

Figure 2.15: House compound of a family engaged in home-weaving. l) Working and dwelling house, veranda with dining area; 2) Weaving room with ATBM loom; 3) Bedroom-cum-workroom for *songkèt*; 4) Bedroom; 5) Sanctuary with abodes of the gods; 6) Open kitchen.

☐ ATBM loom

— *cagcag* loom

⊠ Bed

⊗ Bobbin wheel

Cow

Goat

Hedge

0 1 2 3 4 m

retrained on ATBM looms in a free conversion course which takes only a few days. Meanwhile they have given proof of their skill. Fourteen women still work at home in Gianyar for the entrepreneur, likewise four men apply the tyings for pre-determined patterns at home. After the patterned weft yarn has been dyed, the tyings have to be removed before it can be woven. This removal work is contracted out as home-work, usually to boys who work part-time while they are still attending school.

There are five women weavers working at home in Sidemen for this manufactory—married women over 25 years of age who already have large families and cannot absent themselves from home for the whole day. The manufactory has still not acquired the cold, impersonal atmosphere of a proper factory, and a great deal is still informal. One weaving woman sometimes brings her little son with her to work when she has no one to leave him with. Any worker failing to fulfill his or her quota will know about it on payday, as wages are paid per meter of woven material and according to quality.

The entrepreneur's risk and input were and are considerable, for changes on the market affect him directly. Prices have a marked tendency to plummet, and sales are dependent on the vagaries of fashion. The manufactory's production figures for 1988, for example, are only half what they were in 1983. The owner has been able to ride out the crisis by introducing new designs, particularly motifs from old Balinese and east Indonesian cloths. More recently, brightly-colored red checked fabrics without *endek* have been particularly successful on the market.

Thus, the entrepreneur has prospered. With no land of his own to begin with, he has been able to buy rice and vegetable fields over the course of the years, and to employ others to farm them for him. He owns two rice mills in the village, two house compounds, and a house in a suburb of Denpasar where he goes in his car on business or to visit his older children, who are receiving higher education there. However, as we have noted, the manufactories shave their prices very finely and competition between them is fierce. A single mistake in color, pattern or material, and all that he possesses could be at stake.

HOME-WORK: FAMILY AND COMMISSION WEAVING

The second example deals with a family where the mother is engaged in home-work. The house compound of this particular family is a small complex standing on leased land which belongs to the village temple (see Fig. 2.15). The married couple pay off the lease by working for the temple. They live together with their six children in a house where they also work, and which they built themselves with help from neighbors. They are members of the lower class (like 95 percent of the Balinese population, although the modern money economy with its new opportunities of accumulating wealth is bringing about changes in the previously rigid hierarchic order). One of the three rooms in the house is set aside for *endek* work, and the ATBM loom occupies almost the entire room. In the middle room the 15-year-old daughter and the mother weave *songkèt*. The *cagcag* looms occupy a relatively small space.

The father has leased small plots of land, on which he plants maize and vegetables. If there is no work to do in the fields, he does occasional work in the market, helping to load and unload goods and running errands. He regularly takes his two cows to graze along a grassy roadside or on a tiny pasture. He also looks after the goat and tends to the small-scale gardens within the compound. The oldest child, a son, is already employed part-time as a tyer in an *endek* workshop although he is still attending school.

Before her family became so large, the mother worked for seven-and-a-half years in a small workshop. For the past two-and-a-half years she has had an ATBM loom at home on loan from her previous employer, for whom she continues to work.

The home-worker rises each day shortly before dawn, attending to her large family before the children—ages 6 to 18—go off to school. One of her jobs is also to fetch water (although the eldest daughter sometimes does this for her). From 8 to 10 a.m. she works at the ATBM, and then sees to her housework, goes shopping and prepares the midday meal. At 1 p.m. she returns to the loom for another two hours, after which she must once again tend to domestic chores. After the evening meal she sits down at the *cagcag* loom from 7 to 10 p.m. to weave *songkèt*. The aim of this work, she tells us, is to obtain some (relative) freedom for herself. She wants to earn enough money to buy yarn and gold threads for work which she elects, so that she will not be under the pressure of total dependance upon an employer—at least not in this field. Her hope is to work as an independent producer at least for a few months of the year, but this does not always work out. When school fees and electricity bills have to be paid, there is no money left for new investments and, without these, independance is unattainable. And her exertions begin all over again.

—*B. Hauser-Schäublin and M.L. Nabholz-Kartaschoff*

CHAPTER THREE

Songkèt

Golden Threads, Caste and Privilege

WITH their shimmering splashes of gold and silver threads, *songkèt* cloths are intended for the grand gesture—for public theatrical performances and ceremonial displays of status and wealth. During the heyday of the highly centralized kingdom of Gèlgèl in the 16th century, dance and theater performances were held in the palace forecourt and the open square in front of it, where they could be observed by everyone present. Here the splendor and cultural ideals of the nobility were presented in stylized poses, the players grandly arrayed in sumptuous *songkèt* garments and finely carved masks. The same costumes can be seen today in theatrical performances, in temple and death ceremonies for the nobility, and particularly at tooth-filing and wedding ceremonies—all of which are conceived on a grand theatrical scale and celebrated by participants in splendid costumes (*payas ageng*) with garments of glittering *songkèt* and *perada*. It is easy to imagine on these occasions that one is witnessing reincarnations of Rama and Sita, or Arjuna and Suprabha—characters from the ancient Indian epics with whom the Balinese kings very much identified themselves (Figs. 3.5, 3.6).

Not only in Bali, but throughout the whole of western Indonesia, *songkèt* is the term used to describe a technique in which additional patterns are woven into a material with supplementary weft threads, either running across the entire width or covering only individual parts of the cloth. The early aristocratic *songkèt* textiles (Figs. 3.1, 3.2, 3.4, 3.14, 3.15) consisted entirely of silk. Less sumptuous products intended for theater and dance costumes (Fig. 3.8) were made of cotton, and during the past thirty years of rayon and artificial silk. Today, save for a few rare and prohibitively expensive examples made of pure silk, mixed cloths of silk with artificial silk or viscose are normally seen. Gimp golden and silver threads, colored silk and artificial silk are used as supplementary wefts. Virtually all these materials must be imported from Java, Japan, China, Singapore or India and may be purchased in the large city markets, sometimes also in smaller village stores and markets. The high cost of the raw materials accounts for about three-quarters of the value of a finished cloth.

A GLIMPSE OF HISTORY

The art of *songkèt* is closely associated with Bali's traditional kingdoms and royal families, and a brief historical overview will help us understand the present situation. The first sculptures and documents to throw

Figure 3.1 (opposite and above): *Songkèt* shoulder cloth depicting heads of the demon Kalarau, who is thought to swallow the sun during eclipses. Silk and gold thread on silk. Bulèlèng, early 20th century. 169 x 50 cm. MEB IIc 20780.

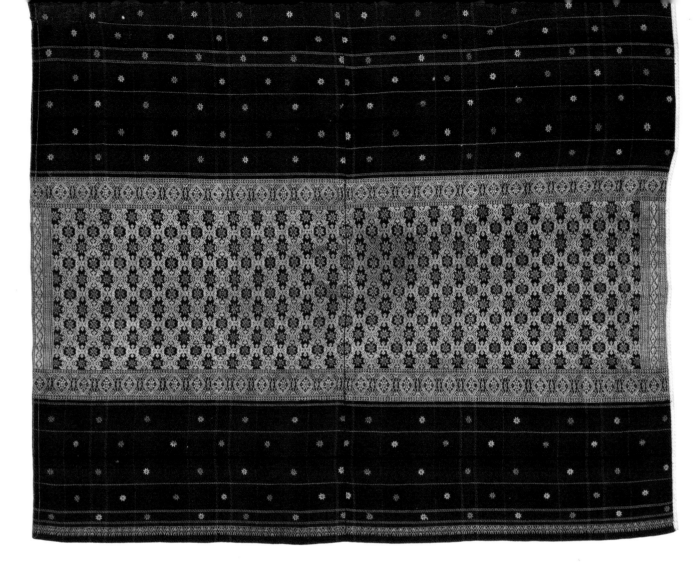

some light on early Balinese history go back to the 8th and 9th centuries A.D., though they cannot be dated exactly. In the 7th century, however, we understand that an international community of over a thousand Buddhist monks was studying in the center of the powerful kingdom of Sriwijaya, based in the vicinity of modern-day Palembang in southern Sumatra. Buddhist doctrines were spread from here by monks and priests and eventually reached Bali; traces of ancient monasteries and hermitages are still to be seen on the island today, and it is in this period that the earliest Hindu-Buddhist kingdoms arose.

The early rulers of Bali became acquainted by such means with Indian forms of state organization, and through the adoption of Indian beliefs in a divine god-king—substantiated by a large body of epic literature—they clearly hoped to strengthen and consolidate their own power. The rulers of ancient Bali therefore summoned Hindu and Buddhist priests as counselors to their courts, and did their best to assimilate many aspects of Indian culture. It is reasonable to suppose that a knowledge of the lavish textile arts required for grand displays at court—such as silk weaving, red dyeing and *songkèt*—also reached Bali during this period. Technical influences thus came directly from India as well as from Palembang (Sriwijaya)—itself a stronghold of *songkèt* production ever since.

Whereas the first royal decrees—the earliest dating from A.D. 882—are in the ancient Balinese language, documents appearing after A.D. 989 are in ancient Javanese and evidence an increasing Javanization of the courts. This date marks the beginning of the twelve-year joint reign of Bali and East Java by King Udayana of Bali—scion of the Warmadéwa dynasty—and Queen Gunapriya of East Java, who has gone down in

Figure 3.2: *Songkèt* hip cloth for women of the nobility, checkered with a star pattern (*polèng bebintangan*). Gold threads on silk. Karangasem, c. 1900. 188 x 124 cm. MEB IIc 19970.

Balinese history as a Tantric magician. The pronounced Javanization of Balinese court society under the reign of their two sons, Airlangga and Anak Wungsu, no doubt strongly influenced relations between the court and the ancient Balinese villages. The latter, it may be supposed, paid dues and rendered services to ruling houses, but were excluded from the royal Tantric rites and burial cults.

In 1343, Bali was occupied by troops from the East Javanese kingdom of Majapahit. Gajah Mada, Majapahit's great minister of state, had brought the kingdom to the zenith of its power, and his military campaign now broke the hegemony of the Balinese rajas. To establish Majapahit claims to sovereignty on a more durable basis, he at once installed a vassal in Bali—a local ruler who until 1398 was totally dependent upon the grace and favor of the Majapahit king.

The first of these vassals was the Brahman Sri Krsna Kapakisan, who set up a court in Samprangan, near Gianyar. Because of his role as a temporal leader, Kapakisan changed his caste to that of a *ksatria* and became the progenitor of the Ksatria Dalem, who still point with pride to their Brahmanic origins. The Javanese imperial administrators who held sway over Bali at that time were members of a somewhat lower stratum of the *ksatria* caste, namely the Ksatria Jawa—or, as their descendants still call themselves today, the Arya.

A FLOWERING OF COURTLY ARTS AND CRAFTS

During the reign in Majapahit of King Hayam Wuruk (A.D. 1350-1389), the brother of the vassal ruling at Samprangan left and founded a new palace (*keraton*) farther to the east, in Gèlgèl near Klungkung. He adopted the title of I Déwa Ketut Tegal Besung, and it seems that from the outset this *keraton* counted among its attendants a large number of literary men, actors, musicians, artists and craftsmen. In the service of the court, they encouraged the spread of Javanese culture throughout the realm, which was for the new rulers a means of influencing the inhabitants. Culture and art now appeared in the new guise of an ideology of power whose protagonists identified themselves with the divine heroes of the Hindu-Javanese epics, and assumed their earthly roles in splendid scenes in which they appeared dressed and adorned as gods.

Gèlgèl eventually became the dominant kingdom on Bali, a centralized realm that ruled most of the island. At the turn of the 16th century, the reign of Dalem Batu Renggong of Gèlgèl brought a period of peace and prosperity in which the Javano-Balinese system of the four castes (*catur wangsa*) was consolidated, and in which art and culture flourished. The king and his priestly teacher, the renowned counselor and court poet Nirartha, made extensive efforts to popularize court art through active encouragement of artistic activities. There was in Gèlgèl, as a result, great enthusiasm for theater and literature—shared not only by Javanese aristocrats but also by local students and aficionados attracted to the court as songwriters, actors and musicians. A whole range of specialized artists and craftsmen produced works of religious edification and royal entertainment. In addition to poets, scribes, dancers and musicians, the entourage included copper, gold and silversmiths, painters, carvers and carpenters—all housed in special quarters near the palace.

Aristocratic women were barred from the exercise of the *pancagina* or

manly arts and crafts, but like women elsewhere in the archipelago were permitted or even required to weave, and thus made their own important contributions to the pomp and circumstance of the court. The production of delicately embroidered and figured cloths with supplementary gold and silver wefts—cloths known as *songkèt*—was their exclusive domain until quite recently. And despite the fact that it has long ceased to be an important political center, the small village of Gèlgèl today remains an important center of *songkèt* production.

DEMOCRATIZATION OF A STATUS SYMBOL

After the 16th century, frequent armed disputes erupted and political power became increasingly diffused. Smaller courts and palaces arose in many areas and grew into independent centers of artistic activity—including *songkèt* production. These included Tabanan, Negara, Mengwi, Bulèlèng and Karangasem.

Among others, the village of Sidemen in eastern Bali developed into a *songkèt* center due to its close connections with the courts of Gèlgèl, Klungkung and Karangasem. During the reign of Batu Renggong, the governor Kyai Singharsa—progenitor of the most important noble line of Sidemen—was sent to Cabola (today *désa adat* Tabola, Sidemen), in order to govern a territory given the name of Singharsa and extending to Tianyar on the north coast. He was accompanied by a priestly acolyte and counselor, Pedanda Mambal, who founded a Brahman settlement known as Sukaton in the proximity of Cabola. The minister responsible for the territory of Singharsa was the eldest son of the reigning monarch, I Déwa Anom Pamayun, who also moved his abode here from Gèlgèl in 1641 accompanied by his own priestly counselor, Pedanda Wayan

Figure 3.3: *Songkèt* cloths with demon heads (*boma*), monkeys, female figures and the two monkey twins Sugriwa and Subali drawn from the Ramayana epic. Colored rayon threads on silk. Karangasem or west Lombok (Balinese), 1920-30. 280 x 83 cm. MEB IIC 19982.

Buruan. The main town of the growing kingdom was then given the name Siddhaman—a name which identified it as a place with a favorable climate, that was particularly esteemed by Brahmans as a place of meditation.

Siddhaman was also apparently well-suited to the strenuous and exacting programming of *songkèt* patterns—demonstrated by the fact that the female descendants of Wayan Buruan, female Brahmans of the Carik and Ulah priestly compounds (the former Sukaton), still possess a special skill in this art. Another focus of *songkèt* production was in the princely estates of the Ksatria Dalem in Siddhaman, Jero Gedé and Jero Kanginan, where the former rulers of Singharsa and later administrators (*punggawa*) resided by favor of the king of Karangasem. It has remained the main center of *songkèt* production ever since.

Thus, from the historical point of view, *songkèt* weaving in Bali has been connected throughout the centuries with the highest castes. The noble ladies and daughters of the courts, and the women of the *gria* or Brahmanic houses, were the sole practitioners of this craft and worked almost exclusively to supply their own needs—for *songkèt* was, of course, a prerogative and mark of distinction for the upper castes.

However, with the economic changes of the last two decades, and the increased democratization of Balinese society that has accompanied them, the claim of the *triwangsa* or three upper castes to such exclusive symbols has been broken. Moreover, the call by former governor Ida Bagus Mantra in 1980 for the Balinese to give preference to traditional textiles in buying their *adat* (ceremonial) cloths has had the unintended effect of neutralizing the former use of such fabrics as marks of high

Figure 3.4 (following pages): Half of a princely outer hip cloth depicting the god Wisnu, the monkey king Hanuman, the demon king Rawana and the *penasar* character from the *wayang*, Twalen. Gold and silver threads on silk. Bulèlèng, c. 1900. 135 x 6l cm. MEB IIc 19968.

social status. Anyone who has acquired some sort of position in Balinese society today, and can afford to buy them, is now authorized to display his or her status at religious and social functions through the use of *songkèt*. Thus *songkèt* has become an integral part of the ceremonial wardrobe of all well-to-do Balinese people.

BALINESE FESTIVE DRESS

The festive apparel of the Balinese consists of a number of lengths of cloth of various sizes, which are never tailored but rather draped, wrapped and tied around the body with great artistry. On ritual occasions, both men and women are only allowed to wear flat, woven pieces of fabric and never tube skirts that have been sewn together at the ends (*sarung*). The latter are worn only as everyday clothing.

Balinese women traditionally wrap their lower body in two long hip cloths—an inner and an outer one—which both reach down at least to the calves, and often to the ankles. The inner of these cloths is worn as an underskirt or *tapih* (*sinjang* in high Balinese). This is wrapped in such a way that the lower, outer end hangs down on the left-hand side of the body. The upper end is pulled out of the top edge of the cloth, hugging the body, and tucked back into it. This underskirt is normally only worn on solemn occasions such as processions, weddings and puberty ceremonies. In former times, it was customary at puberty and tooth-filing ceremonies that such underskirts should consist of ritually prescribed cloths such as *cepuk* or *padang derman*, and the part of the underskirt that shows when walking is said to have formerly consisted of a strip of silk sewn on to the end of two joined lengths of cotton. Today, simple printed cottons are often worn, as well as *perada* cloths of the kind that can be bought at the local market.

Over this inner hip cloth, a much more elaborately worked outer wraparound cloth is worn, known as a *kamben* (high Balinese *wastra*). This is passed around the body one and a half times and extends from the waist to the ankles. It is wrapped as tightly as possible and secured at the waist on the left side, at about hip level, or else in front at the center. Precious cloths, especially *songkèt* pieces which have become quite stiff by the addition of gold and silver threads, must as a result be more loosely wound.

Figure 3.5 (left): Noble tooth-filing candidates in rich *songkèt* and *perada* wardrobe, produced in their own *puri*. Tabanan, Belayu.

Figure 3.6 (right): Brahmans preparing their instruments and a spittoon for a tooth-filing ceremony. The bed for the candidates is richly decorated with *perada* cloth and a rare silk *cepuk* with *perada*. Tabanan, Belayu.

The outer wraparound cloth is secured by long narrow sashes, sometimes as well by safety pins. On festive occasions, a long narrow band, often black, is wrapped tightly several times around the body, serving as a kind of corset. Over this is worn a colored sash, often adorned with gold leaf or bronze paint, known as a *sabuk* (high Balinese *pakekek*), which almost completely covers the corset below. On particularly solemn occasions, this band is worn as a broad shawl draping in a spiral from the hips to the breast line.

The traditional feminine upper garment consists of a breast cloth of variable size which is wrapped tightly round the upper body, known as an *anteng*. Narrower breast cloths leave the shoulders free, but larger *seléndang* might also be wound round the upper body and thrown over one shoulder. Until the 1930s, Balinese women customarily went about with their upper bodies naked. At temple festivals or on solemn occasions celebrated by the nobility in the *puri* (palace) or *jero* (princely house) or by the Brahmans in the *gria*, the *kamben cerik* or *seléndang* was drawn up over the breast, that is to say, worn as an *anteng* or breast cloth. While the traditional bare-shoulder dress is still worn at temple festivals and life-cycle ceremonies, it has been replaced today in many parts of Bali by the long-sleeved Javanese *kebaya* blouse which is frequently made of a lacey material.

In contrast to the female attire, the *adat* clothing of men consists of a wraparound cloth or *kamben* (high Balinese *wastra*) serving as a waist cloth which reaches down to the knees or just below. The cloth is first passed around the waist from behind; the two free ends are then draped so that one tip (the *kancut*, high Balinese *lancingan*) swings loosely, almost touching the ground.

At major festivals of the nobility and Brahmans, a second, narrower cloth (*saput*, high Balinese *kampuh*) is worn over the inner hip cloth; it consists of two widths of woven fabric sewn together, with decorative borders (*tepi*) about four centimeters wide on either edge. Both cloths are secured with a belt-like sash or *sabuk* (high Balinese *pakekek*). Members of the higher castes are permitted by sartorial tradition to pull a joined double width of *songkèt* or *perada* cloth over the chest and up to the armpits, and to knot it with a band of fabric (*umpal*). Nowadays it is more common to wear only one width as an outer hip cloth, together

Figure 3.7 (left): Bridal couple in *songkèt* dress. Karangasem, Sidemen.

Figure 3.8 (right): *Topèng* dancer with outer hip cloth of cotton *songkèt*. Karangasem, Ipah.

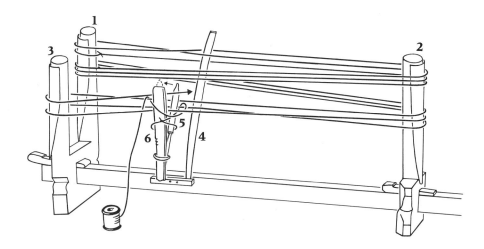

Figure 3.9: Warping device. **1**) and **3**) fixed vertical wooden pegs; **2**) movable wooden peg; **4**) bamboo stick for making the warping lease; **5**) bamboo slat for making the lease bar shed; **6**) palm leaf for making the heddle rod shed and the heddle loops.

with a western or Indonesian national-style batik shirt. Instead of the former square headcloths with *songkèt* patterns which had to be wrapped around the head (*udeng*, high Balinese *destar*), and whose patterns differed from one principality to another, men now often wear boat-shaped headgear which can be bought pre-sewn at the market.

AN EXTREMELY SPECIALIZED CRAFT

The *songkèt* production process is complicated and time-consuming. Certain stages are executed by assistants or specialists, or jointly undertaken with other women, thereby incurring additional costs for the weaver and further reducing her already slender profit. As a rule, her earnings are no more than about twenty percent of the final price the material fetches at market.

First the yarns must be wound from purchased hanks onto small bamboo bobbins—a time-consuming job which is frequently taken over by elder members of the family. Next, the plain or striped warp is prepared, either by the weaver herself or by a specialist (Fig. 3.10). It takes about fifteen hours of work to prepare a warp for three hip cloths. The warping device (*penganyinan*) consists of a long horizontal beam with three vertical wooden pegs (see Fig. 3.9). Two of these pegs (1 and 3) are fixed, whereas the third (2) can be moved according to the length of the warp. The warp threads are wound to and fro round the pegs from a revolving bobbin. As with any simple weaving device, the *songkèt* loom basically requires the arrangement of a lease, keeping even and odd warp threads in good order, and two sheds (lease bar shed and heddle rod shed) for the alternate lifting of the even and the odd thread sets. During warping, the lease is formed around the bamboo stick (4), the lease bar shed near the cane sliver (5), and the heddle rod shed and the heddle loops near the palm leaf (6). The warp is then fixed at various places to prevent the warp threads from becoming tangled, and with the addition of the warp beam and the various sticks for shedding, it is rolled up into a bundle and handed over to the programming specialist.

Setting up the additional heddle rods for pattern programming (*nuduk*) is by far the most exacting process in the whole production. The demands on the woman's dexterity, patience and eyesight are so great that only a few specialists perform this task. The best programmers are said to be certain Brahman women and gifted weavers from the *puri* and *jero* of the *ksatria* caste. But there are also other women who have learned this exacting craft, and who work on their own account or accept commissions.

The most important part of the loom for weaving the supplementary weft pattern is at the rear in the warp. Setting it up is the job of the programmer. First she stretches the warp supplied and draws each warp thread individually through the spaces in the reed. Referring to an old cloth, a woven sample (*tulad*), or a model of sticks and yarn with a pattern repeat, she now counts the warp threads for the first pattern weft by hand with the aid of a small bamboo slat (9), and inserts a thin palm leaf rod or a plastic strip (Fig. 3.12). She proceeds weft thread by weft thread until the whole of the pattern repeat has been counted. Then each strip is replaced by a rod with heddle loops (11) with which the appropriate groups of weft threads can be lifted during the weaving process. The whole bundle of pattern heddle rods—as many as 120 or more with large patterns—is finally pushed to the rear of the warp. This arrangement has to be made for each new warp, which suffices for making three hip cloths or eight to ten *seléndang*. Depending on the width of the cloth, the fineness of the yarn, and the pattern repeat, a *nuduk* specialist needs one to two days and is relatively badly paid.

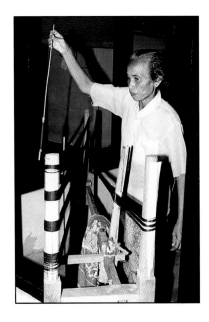

The warp bundle now goes to the weaving woman's compound. To give the reader a better understanding of the weaving process, the following is a short description of the traditional *cagcag* or backstrap loom (see Fig. 3.11). Used also for weaving other types of material, it was once (and to some extent still is) widely employed in Bali. The name *cagcag* reproduces onomatopoeically the sound made when the weaver shoots the weft through the warp with a regular rhythm. There is hardly a village in Bali in which the familiar clatter cannot be heard emanating from enclosed compounds. Typologically, the Balinese *cagcag* belongs to a category of backstrap looms found also in Sumatra and Java. This loom can produce only cloths of a limited width; for this reason, large cloths necessarily consist of two widths sewn together.

The flat, discontinuous warp is stretched taut between a board-shaped warp beam (12) in two sturdy forked posts (13) at the back and the breast-cum-cloth beam (2) at the front. The weaver sits on the ground and secures the breast beam firmly to herself by means of a wooden yoke (1; Fig. 3.13). She can brace her outstretched legs against a horizontal crossbeam (14) supporting the warp frame. The entire weight rests on her back and she can tauten and relax the warp during work by shifting her weight backwards and forwards, which requires a great deal of strength and practice.

Freely inserted in the warp are the various components for the weaving process: the reed of bamboo (5) and the solid wooden sword stick (6) which are used together to beat the weft into place, and heddle rod and lease bar (7 and 8) for creating the ground sheds for plain weaving. The sword stick is turned on its side to enlarge these sheds for the insertion of the shuttle (3), and then withdrawn after each beat-up and placed obliquely on the rest (15).

As a rule, three ground picks alternate with three supplementary wefts.

Figure 3.10: Warping the plain-colored threads. Karangasem, Sidemen.

Figure 3.11: The *cagcag* loom. **1**) yoke (*por*); **2**) breast-cum-cloth beam (*apit*); **3**) shuttle with weft (*peleting*); **4**) small pieces of cardboard with gold thread; **5**) reed (*serat*); **6**) sword stick (*belida*); **7**) heddle rod (*jeriring* with *guun gedé*); **8**) lease bar (*seleran*); **9**) bamboo slat for opening pattern sheds (*sorog*); **10**) thin palm-leaf pattern rods (*gilik*); **11**) pattern heddle rods (*gegilik* with *guun*); **12**) warp beam (*pandalan*); **13**) warp beam frame (*galeng cagcag*); **14**) crossbeam for bracing legs; **15**) rest for sword stick (*rorogan*).

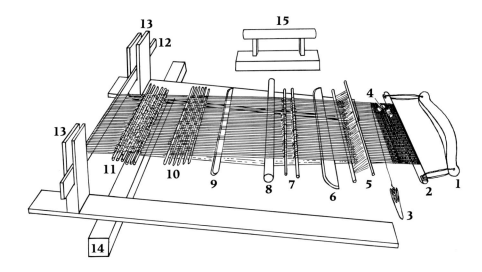

The latter are wound up on small pieces of cardboard. The cloth lies in the loom in such a way that the patterns can be seen from the back and the thread ends can be knotted. For supplementary wefts, the weaver lifts the individual pattern heddle rods (11) and again inserts thin palm-leaf rods (10) for a whole repeat, drawing these toward her little by little and one at a time, using the bamboo slat to enlarge the pattern shed. After the three supplementary wefts have been inserted, the slat is withdrawn and it is the next thin palm-leaf rod's turn. A direct lifting and weaving with the pattern heddle rods is impossible; they would become tangled, and errors might find their way into the pattern. The weaving process is a slow and tedious one, and it will be appreciated that a weaver, however deft, needs at least five days for a simple *seléndang*, and up to a month or more for a hip cloth with a complicated pattern.

Basically all *cagcag* looms and technical processes in Bali are the same, though there are some local variations. In Gèlgèl the looms are much more sturdily built than elsewhere—the sword stick is longer and heavier, and the voluminous bundles of pattern heddle rods are suspended from the warp beam frame. Much the same is to be seen in Negara and in Beratan (Bulèlèng). In every case this is due to the fact that finer and denser *songkèt* cloths with very large pattern repeats are made.

On the other hand, several villages in Bulèlèng and Tabanan have started to develop *cagcag* looms for small widths of cloth, at which the weaver does not sit on the ground, but perches more comfortably on a small stool or fixed bench. A loom was also invented for weaving two or up to three narrow cloths in parallel. So far, however, there has been no modernization or rationalization of the complicated patterning process. This would require complex mechanical equipment which no home weaver could afford. Moreover, freedom in the choice of pattern would be seriously curtailed, which would be quite contrary to the spirit of the weavers and their delight in variety.

REGIONAL SONGKÈT STYLES

As is the case with *endek* cloths, various historical linkages among the former Balinese principalities make it difficult for us today to clearly distinguish regional styles of *songkèt*. This is especially true since the earliest extant specimens are scarcely more than a hundred years old. The dividing lines are extremely fluid, as transpositions of particular styles across regional boundaries by way of feudal and family connections have been the rule. In conversations with older *ksatria* women of Bulèlèng, Klungkung, Karangasem and Tabanan—undoubtedly the most knowledgeable sources on this subject—one and the same *songkèt* is often assigned a variety of origins. Aesthetic tastes, moreover, are quite variable and localized. In the village of Patemon, north Bali, for example, the Pandé Beratan weavers assert that their *songkèt* are the most beautiful, and they consider Beratan to be the place of origin of the craft. In Gèlgèl it is much the same story: "Our *songkèt* are the best in the whole of Bali, and together with Karangasem, this is the home of these cloths." But in Tabanan and Negara (Jembrana) as well, *songkèt* materials of outstanding quality were once produced.

With reference to some pictures of old and particularly typical specimens of varying origins, a first attempt can be made at identifying some local characteristics of earlier times. *Songkèt* cloths from Bulèlèng dating back to the turn of the century are notable for their deep brownish reds, purples and occasional violets, and for their frequent combination of gold with silver threads. In most cloths, the center field is covered with a dense network of crenations, lozenges, stars, blossoms or butterflies, and is framed by a clearly defined border. This usually consists of prominent triangles composed of vegetable elements (Figs. 3.4, 3.13-15). This common motif is frequently called *tetumpengan*, after the cone-shaped sacrificial offerings of cooked rice (*tumpeng*), or *pucuk rebong* after the shape of a young shoot of bamboo. It is still found as a border on many *songkèt* cloths, but is nowhere patterned with such refinement and baroque verve as in Bulèlèng.

A typical feature of Bulèlèng are the pairs of triangles composed into rectangles, which interplay with the contrast between gold threads and a dark red background (Fig. 3.14). There are no clearly established names for patterns. In the eyes of the imaginative makers and users, specific forms summon up an ever-changing range of ideas. This triangular pattern, for example, is called by some *belah ketipat* ("a square rice cake that has been split") and by others *tuung aceh* ("a kind of nightshade or *Solanaceae* plant") and by still others *pepudakan* ("the shape of a kind of *pandanus* palm"). There are many designs consisting of plain-colored or *endek*-patterned bands and *songkèt* strips with delicate cross and lozenge patterns, particularly on breast and shoulder cloths.

Some of the geometrical patterns of Bulèlèng also belong to the classical repertoire of *songkèt* textiles from the princely courts of Karangasem and Klungkung. Karangasem is notable in particular for a deep, warm red and a background checked pattern with fine lines and tiny scattered motifs in the form of stars or blossoms (Fig. 3.2). In the central part of this women's hip cloth, the golden patterns coalesce into a shimmering constellation of stars. Even today checked materials with golden patterns (*songkèt polèng*) are typical of east Bali (Fig. 3.13).

Figure 3.12 (top): Programming the pattern heddle rods (*nuduk*). Karangasem, Sidemen.

Figure 3.13 (above): Young *ksatria* women weaving a checkered *songkèt polèng* with *tumpeng* border for an outer hip cloth. Karangasem, Sidemen.

Figure 3.14 (following pages): Princely *songkèt* outer hip cloth. Gold and silver threads on silk. Bulèlèng, c. 1900. 142 x 116 cm. MEB IIc 19967.

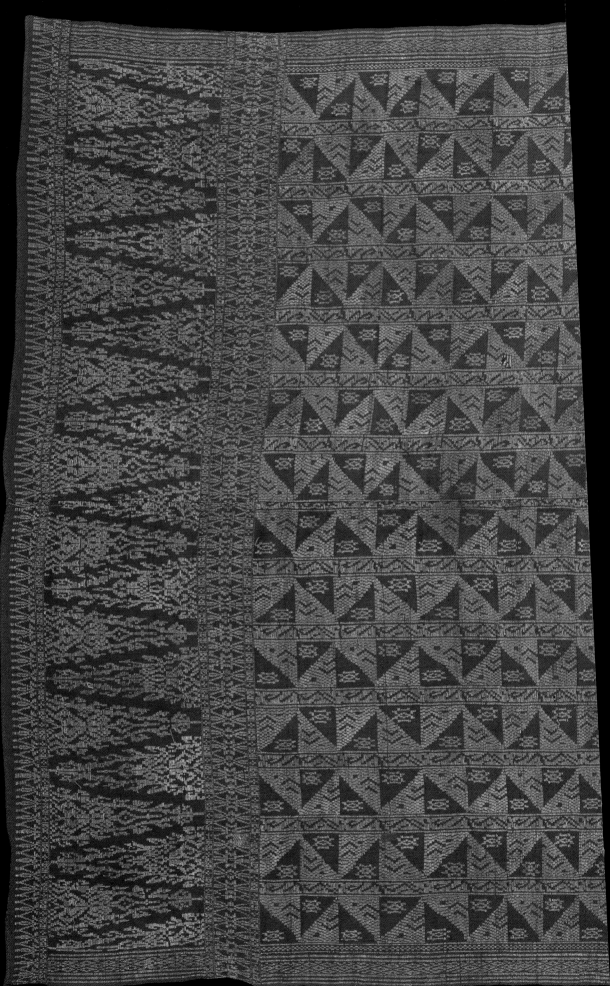

Extremely delicate *songkèt* textiles with tiny lozenges and stars almost completely covering the surface of a hip cloth, or arranged in multicolored strips on breast cloths, were once woven in the *puri* of Tabanan and Kerambitan. Stylistically, they recall more vividly than any other Balinese textiles the *songkèt* from Aceh and Palembang in Sumatra. Whereas in the past almost every member of a princely family knew how to weave *songkèt*, the tradition has now almost died out. In Belayu, a small village near the town of Tabanan, however, the weaving of *songkèt* continues to flourish.

Songkèt fabrics from Klungkung show close affinities with those of Karangasem. Typical of these, it is said, are the rather short and broad triangular forms in the borders which, although finely woven, are chunkier than in Karangasem or Bulèlèng. Materials from Klungkung and Sidemen of more recent date are striking because of their complex, curvilinear bird motifs, which may harken back to earlier originals.

Early depictions of gods, demons and mythological figures are very rare, and constitute some of the highlights of Karangasem *songkèt* weavings (Fig. 3.4). Figural patterns were also woven in addition to geometrical designs in the west Balinese princely court of Negara (Fig. 3.15). However, they are done in a much thicker gold thread, and the style of composition is somewhat stiff.

In the 1920s and '30s, an increasing number of *songkèt* cloths were produced with patterned parts in color made of silk, and later rayon. Tabanan became famous for *songkèt* textiles with large figurative patterns and flowering tendrils; other characteristic Tabanan cloths combine

Figure 3.15: Breast or shoulder cloth with *naga* snakes. Gold threads on silk. Jembrana, Negara, first half of the 20th century. 150 x 43 cm.
MEB IIc 19962.

stripes with fine *songkèt* and *endek* patterns in orange, green and violet. Fig. 3.3 shows another artistically designed example from this period. It probably came from Karangasem or from the neighboring island of Lombok, which was ruled by Karangasem in the 17th and 18th centuries; its west coast is still settled by large numbers of Balinese. Their *songkèt* textiles are distinguished in general by a very finely woven style which is a little on the stiff side.

If woven samples (*tulad*) used by programmers as mnemonic aids to set up looms from various regions are compared, it will be found that what were once strictly local patterns are now found throughout Bali. At supraregional markets, particularly in the bazaars of the capital, *songkèt* cloths from many parts of Bali are sold: from Klungkung, Sidemen and other villages in Karangasem, from Negara, from Belayu (Tabanan) and from Singaraja and its environs. Production centers near Singaraja which are renowned for the best quality are the *adat* village of Beratan on the fringes of the city and the similarly named Banjar Beratan in the village of Patemon near Bubunan, where the craft has long been firmly in the hands of the wives of traditional silver and goldsmiths, the Pandé Beratan. Today regional differences are to be found less in the composition of the patterns than in the quality of the raw materials and the weaving technique, and, accordingly, in the price.

As already described in the previous chapter, depending on their economic situation *songkèt* weavers today work on their own or for dealers. Distribution of finished products is frequently in the hands of former weavers who have become entrepreneurs. Thus the most capable dealer in a village in Karangasem was previously famed as an excellent *songkèt* weaver who could program patterns for herself and other women. Beginning in the 1950s, she started retailing *songkèt* materials as a sideline, and covered long distances as an itinerant merchant—going to Klungkung and as far as Denpasar. Today the exacting weaving work is too much for her because of eye trouble, and she devotes herself entirely to trading. She has more than a hundred home weavers working for her, sometimes almost as indentured laborers, and she sells their products in her own shop in the village, as well as at the big markets in Klungkung and in the capital. Intermediate dealers and ultimate vendors cream off about a quarter of the final sales in profit. Weaving women from Brahman and *ksatria* families are, as a rule, less dependent on this system, and frequently produce to order. The first cooperatives have now developed, the earliest being in west Bali; some are planned in north Bali.

In spite of the weavers' low income, genuine *songkèt* cloths are too expensive for many people. Consequently, golden machine-woven cloths made from cheap Lurex material, and screen-printed textiles with imitated *songkèt* patterns, are appearing in ever greater quantities at markets, festivals and ceremonies, so that even poorer Balinese need not deny themselves the prestige of textiles that were once the prerogative of the nobility.

—*U. Ramseyer and M.L. Nabholz-Kartaschoff*

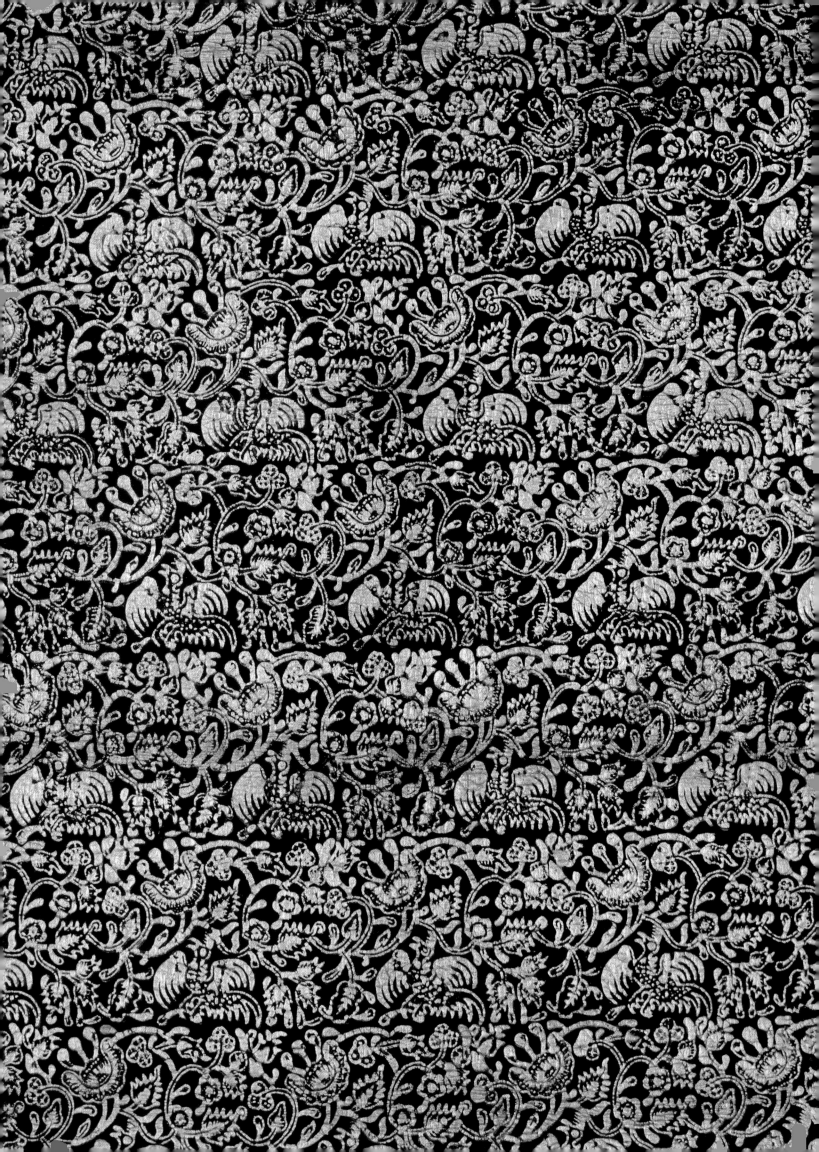

CHAPTER FOUR

Perada

Gilded Garments for Humans, Gods and Temples

THE curtain opens. *Tua*, the old man, steps out furtively, nosing around the stage. He is one of the most popular figures in the *topèng* masked dance drama, and the comical way that he plucks at his *kampuh* in embarrassment invariably sets the audience roaring (Fig. 4.4). This broad, stiff wraparound cloth, worn over an undergarment, is sewn together from pieces of brightly colored cotton material and decorated with opulent gold patterns—it is called a *kampuh perada*.

In Bali, *perada* is the name given to the technique whereby cotton (or more rarely, silk) is adorned with gold leaf or gold dust. Today the effect is usually produced by applying bronze pigment paints or plastic gold foil. The base fabric consists of simple plain, striped or checked cloths in brilliant colors (crimson, orange, blue, violet, and also black) against which the gold patterns stand out conspicuously. A white background with gold yields a more delicate, but no less pleasing combination.

PERADA PATTERNS AND MATERIALS

Since no weaving is involved, the designer has a much freer hand with *perada* designs than with most other patterned textiles, and can produce interlaced motifs and rounded forms. The most common patterns are large lotus blossoms and other flowers, winding tendrils and leaves (for example, the one illustrated on the book's jacket), triangular *tumpal* designs with lines or plant elements, phoenixes and other birds of every kind, as well as figures from the *wayang* shadow-play drama. The inventory of motifs showing Chinese influences includes the popular *banji* patterns (Figs. 4.2, 4.4) which create a network of swastikas, meanders and interlocking tees in panels and border frames. This whole style of patterning bears a surprising resemblance to certain carved architectural details, which are also frequently gilded, or to golden paper decorations like scissor cuts found on cremation towers and caskets (Fig. 1.15).

Batik materials from Java, with white motifs on indigo blue or vice versa, were once commonly used as a base fabric. As a rule they came from the north coast, some also from Central Java, and had patterns characteristic of these batik production centers, such as rosettes, lozenges, stars, intertwined tendrils and geometrically stylized wings. The gold ornamentation then usually outlined the contours or accentuated the internal pattern of individual motifs. But there are also some highly

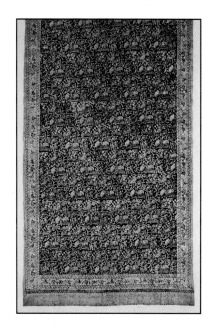

Figure 4.1 (opposite and above): *Seléndang perada*. Javanese cotton batik as base fabric. Bali, early 20th century. 320 x 75 cm. MEB IIc 16117.

Figure 4.2: *Destar batik perada,* men's headcloth. Gold leaf on cotton batik from North Java, Rembang, early 20th century. 102 x 102 cm. MEB IIc 16121.

sophisticated forms in which gold ornamentation is placed over the existing batik design to form independent motifs, as in the opulent man's headcloth in Fig. 4.2. There are examples of *songkèt* (Bulèlèng) or *cepuk* (Tabanan) cloths decorated with *perada*, but these are very rare (Fig. 3.6).

In the past, before the gold pattern was applied, the lines or surfaces were marked out with glue (*ancur*) over a preliminary sketch, or else painted on freehand. The whitish *ancur* glue was obtained from fish bones; another brownish glue produced from water buffalo (*kerbau*) skin was also once used—similar to that employed today to gild woodcarvings and leather *wayang* figures. Sometimes the glue was mixed with a certain amount of ruddle so that if any of the rather fragile gold flaked off, the damaged part would be less conspicuous. The ruddle was also credited with giving an enhanced luster to the reddish gleam of the gold. The finest gold leaf or dust was then applied to the adhesive surfaces.

Gold that extended beyond the limits of the pattern could be easily removed with a soft cloth or brush, or by blowing—but the excess was all carefully collected because of its value. There are several names in Bali for genuine *perada* fabrics: *perada gedé* ("big *perada*"), *perada pelpel* ("thin, flat *perada*") or *perada belanda* ("Dutch *perada*," obviously connected with the provenance of the gold or the place of purchase).

This all belongs to the past. Real gold is beyond the means of all but a few, and so today almost all *perada* patterns are painted directly onto the material with cheap, bronze pigment paint (*perada air*, "water *perada*"). The young Brahman from Kusamba in Fig. 4.3 learned the technique in an aristocratic compound in Klungkung. Today he accepts commissions to decorate banners, ceremonial parasols, hangings of all kinds (*ider-ider*, *langsé*), fans for dancing girls and for decorative purposes or, as in this case, garments for effigies of the divinities. He mixes gold bronze powder with thinner and contact adhesive, and with no drawing to go by he applies the patterns freehand with a brush onto fine cotton material or inexpensive synthetic fabrics—all of which he buys in the large market in nearby Klungkung. He must work deftly and expeditiously before the mixture dries up. A new and more expensive modern method consists of transferring artificial gold plastic foil (*perada plastik*) onto patterns previously applied with red or yellow oil paint.

Perada materials are stiff and brittle where the gold has been applied, the fabrics cannot be washed, and the gold easily rubs off. It is hardly surprising, then, that these opulent textiles are confined to very specific purposes. People wear them only on special occasions as wraparound skirts, breast cloths, sashes and waistbands—as formal attire at tooth-

Figure 4.3 (left): Young brahman painting a wraparound skirt for an effigy of a divinity with bronze pigment paint (*perada air*). Klungkung, Kusamba.

Figure 4.4 (right): *Tua*, the old man, in *topèng* dramas. South Bali, Saba.

filing ceremonies (Fig. 3.5) and weddings, or on other occasions calling for *adat* dress of the very highest grade. This was the case, for example, at an important purification ceremony for the souls of dead ancestors at Sanur, where many women in white wore a piece of colored *perada* material showing under their skirts (Fig. 1.4). They are also the dominant elements in garments worn by dancers. Tightly wound round the upper body with the long ends hanging down in front, they ornament the lithe figures of little *legong* dancers. As broad cloths wrapped around the body with a *keris* stuck in them, they become lively instruments of expression for *topèng* dancers (Fig. 4.4).

Perada cloths are conspicuously present in temple festivals at all levels— as constituents of sacrificial offerings and the underlays on which they are placed, as ceremonial parasols and flags, and as decorative architectural elements. The statues that serve as the receptacles of gods, and the figures of ancestors raised to divine status in rituals, are dressed with tiny wraparound skirts, collars and shoulder cloths made of *perada* materials.

PERADA ORNAMENTATION

Like silk cultivation, red dyeing, and *songkèt* weaving, the technique of gold-leaf decoration, as well as a number of its ornamental patterns, were brought to Java and Bali over the centuries by Indian and Chinese merchants and travelers. Certain passages in Old Javanese written sources suggest that *perada* cloths enjoyed very great popularity in aristocratic circles in the East Javanese kingdom of Majapahit (1293-1478), and that their roots may possibly be traced back to China. Whether there were really *perada* textiles in Bali at such an early date is uncertain, for no extant materials can be dated earlier than the end of the 19th century. As with many other cloths, they were at this time the prerogative of the local princely courts.

Bulèlèng seems to have played a prominent role—we know that *songkèt* cloths with gold add-on were made there, and also that gold leaf was an important article of commerce imported from China and from Siam (Thailand) via the Dutch-controlled port of Singaraja in the latter half of the 19th century. Moreover, an inventory of characteristic *perada* patterns points to links with these civilizations—the geometric *banji* pattern to China, and the entwined plant-and-flower ornaments to the Indo-Chinese peninsula, which was once greatly renowned for its gold-leaf techniques. Other forms appear inspired by European motifs, possibly by Dutch porcelains. On the other hand, the principalities of Karangasem and Klungkung, especially the village of Kamasan, are likely to have been important centers. Even figurative *endek* textiles have been decorated with *perada* there (Fig. 2.11).

In fact, even today the application of *perada* to textiles appears to belong to the same complex of "courtly crafts" as application of gold to leather shadow-theater figures, and to ceremonial objects such as crowns, ornaments on *barong* figures, etc. Unlike *songkèt* weaving and other textile techniques, the craft of making *perada* has always been practiced exclusively by men, and their products were originally restricted to the courts.

Today the situation has changed completely. With the waning of the courts after the Dutch conquests and Indonesian independence, and with Bali's recent economic upsurge, *perada* cloths have gone through a new process of popularization, though at the same time suffering a serious decline in quality. *Perada* is now used everywhere in Bali by all classes of people. Many new production centers (e.g. Sukawati and villages around the town of Klungkung, especially Satria) now manufacture *perada* of a very coarse quality in large quantities, the painting being done exclusively with the help of screens and with bronze pigment paint (*berons mas*). These textiles, however, are but poor imitations of the traditional *perada*.

—*M.L. Nabholz-Kartaschoff*

CHAPTER FIVE

Bebali

Borderlines Between the Sacred and the Profane

D **ENPASAR,** capital of the province of Bali, is a hot and bustling commercial center. Foreigners lacking a compelling reason to be here generally make a detour around the city in search of more scenic destinations elsewhere on the island. But for those with an interest in Balinese culture and religion, a walk through the town can be a worthwhile experience. In addition to the Bali Museum, one can visit the huge Badung market complex which lies in the center of town, on the eastern bank of the river near the intersection of Jl. Gajah Mada with Jl. Sulawesi. Here, on the second floor, the visitor will find a wide range of ceremonial textiles and plaited work, together with a bewildering variety of other accessories intended for use in the complex ritual cycles in which Hindu-Balinese religious beliefs find their physical expression.

The market overflows with ritual paraphernalia of every description: artistically plaited offering covers are displayed alongside bowls, beakers and jugs made of earthenware, aluminum or thin silver sheeting used to make and hold holy water. Brightly-colored parasols, banners and cloth tapestries are offered for sale, as well as cloths used to drape various parts of the temple and house compound, including those that invest the stone and wooden guardian figures with magical potency. Other cloths found here are used to place finishing touches on offerings, or to confer protection and distinction upon the central participants in the rituals. A vibrant, magical energy emanates from black-and-white checked *polèng* cloths (see Chapter 8) stored in large bolts, from which the saleswoman cuts off pieces of the required size.

Amidst this vivid panoply of colors, it is at first easy to overlook a number of narrow, white or patterned bands and sashes, including some with a circular, continuous warp. The latter, which double back on themselves at the fringe, are known in north and south Bali as *wangsul* (meaning "to return" in high Balinese). In eastern Bali, namely in Karangasem and areas of Klungkung, they are also called *gedogan*. These sacred cotton textiles are used primarily in rites of passage, where they form a part of the sacrificial offerings. They also play a key symbolic role in certain other rituals which will be described below.

In addition to these, there are bolts of loosely woven striped or checked materials in various shades, sold as piece goods and worn as part of the *adat* or customary dress of infants during the ceremony marking a

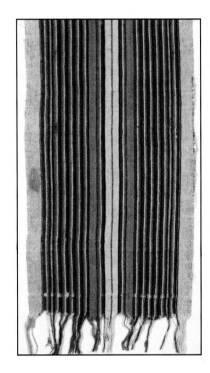

Figure 5.1 (opposite and above): *Wangsul* cloth with uncut warp. Cotton. South Bali. 140 x 35cm. MEB IIc 14047.

change of status 105 days after birth (i.e., after three Balinese months). Depending on the region, this ceremony is known as *nyambutin* ("to receive") or *nelubulanin* ("to celebrate the three months"—*nigang sasihin* in high Balinese). The sacred fabrics used in this ritual, known collectively as *bebali* (a general term applied to ceremonial dances and objects), acquire special significance when the central participant is brought before a priest—that is to say before God—to receive the essence of the offerings and to be purified and dedicated. Depending on their specific colors, swatches of *bebali* cloth can also form part of the ritual dress of the divinity in his tripartite manifestation as Trimurti (Siwa, Wisnu, Brahma)—presented at temple ceremonies as piles of cloth offer-ings (*rantasan, tigasan*).

The Badung market currently offers a total of nine differently patterned *bebali* cloths for such purposes, variously colored and each with its own name. There is, for example, cloth with a white warp and a weft broken by green, red and yellow stripes known as *cenana kawi* ("a type of san-dalwood"). Such 75-centimeter long cloths are worn as wraparounds at the three-month ritual, and are also laid out as part of the divine apparel in the center of the tripartite shrine (*rong tiga*) of an ancestral temple (*pura dadia, paibon* or *pamerajan*). *Bias membah* ("running sand") has a white warp, and a weft in which 8-millimeter gray and white stripes alternate. This cloth, too, is used not only in the three-month ritual but also to decorate the northern compartment of the ancestral shrine in the house compound. *Encakan taluh* ("smashed egg") is a cloth with a vivid red-and-white checked pattern that is brought into the temple as apparel for Brahma, the god residing in the south.

SACRED CLOTH AND RITUAL COMPETENCE

The particular objects and offerings used in rituals depend on the level as well as the type of ceremony being performed. These rituals can be either high (*utama*), medium (*madia*) or low (*nista*), and all have been grouped into five ritual categories (*panca yadnya*) according to their form and purpose. *Déwa yadnya* (rituals for gods) is the term applied to temple rituals having to do with the worship of gods and divine ancestors. *Manusa yadnya* (rituals for humans) are rites directed to the well-being of the living, primarily during critical transitional periods from one stage of life to another (rites of passage). *Pitra yadnya* (rituals for the dead) is a generic term for highly intricate rituals dedicated to the care of the bod-ies and spirits of the deceased. The category *bhuta yadnya* (rituals for ghosts and demons) refers to the pacification or exorcism of forces that might disturb the favorable tenor of affairs. And finally, *resi yadnya* (ritu-als for priests) are rituals performed for the ordination of holy men.

The colors used in ritual objects each have their own symbolism and direction. Yellow and white are assigned to the god Mahadéwa in the west and Iswara in the east, respectively. The two colors may express the complementary dualism of Buddhism and Siwaism, and often indicate the presence of the supreme god Siwa in his bisexual aspect, or in his total hermaphroditic appearance as Ardanaréswari. Red is the color of the creator Brahma, assigned to the south; and black, green or blue are the colors of the preserver Wisnu who rules the north.

The paraphernalia required in the performance of rituals may be pro-vided by the local village or town community (*banjar*), by a temple

Figure 5.2: Under hip cloth *padang derman*. Cotton. South Bali. 167 x 107 cm. MEB IIc 20347.

Figure 5.3 (opposite): Prior to the tooth filing. The *adat* dress of young women consists of a *kamben sekordi barak* and a yellow breast cloth *kalung kuning*. Karangasem.

Figure 5.4 (from top): In the family temple of the Buddhist priests and priestesses three altars have been dressed like human beings. Black is the color for the north; yellow, white and mixed colors determine the center and red stands for the south. Karangasem, Budakeling.

congregation, or by an individual or clan association organizing the ceremony. Those not in a position to produce their own offerings and not able to afford more lavish ritual objects and materials can purchase everything needed for the proper performance of a ceremony conveniently prepared for them and offered for sale at comparatively reasonable prices in the aisles of the Badung market.

The *bebali* cloths sold in the Badung market are produced nearby, in the Pemeregan district, by members of the former princely house of Badung, who also trade in the fabrics. Thus Anak Agung Raka Wartini, an entrepreneur of noble birth, has eight ATBM looms operating in her own house and neighboring compounds, just a few steps behind the fruit market. She provides yarns to the weavers, most of whom are young, and then markets the finished piece goods they produce. There is another production center at Abiantimbul, near Kuta, which makes cheap, modern *bebali* cloths from imported cotton (weft) and viscose (warp) yarns. Here again, production is in the hands of members of the Badung nobility.

In general, it may be said that members of the three high castes (*triwangsa*) have a monopoly over the production of sacred cloths used in rituals. This monopoly is also connected with the monopoly of knowhow in the composition and arrangement of offerings possessed by the *tukang banten*, women who produce offerings for others, and who also come primarily from *Brahmana*, *ksatria* and *wesia* circles. In general, these are the people who know the pattern of a ritual, and who also to some extent determine its form. They alone know where and at what time the correct *wangsul* and *bebali* are to be used.

Although much of this knowledge is oral, palm-leaf manuscripts (*lontar*) do provide written guidelines for the performance of rituals. These texts are in the safekeeping of the priestly and princely families and themselves form part of the cult paraphernalia used in rituals, all of which is brought to the ceremony by the priest or priestess, the *tukang banten* and their retinues, and then taken home again after use.

RELEASING THE BOUND ENERGIES

It is hardly possible today to trace the origin of the continuous-warp *wangsul* with any certainty. There is good reason to believe, however, that this is an indigenous Indonesian textile tradition that was used ritually in the ancient East Javanese kingdom of Majapahit. Of particular interest in this respect is a reference in the 14th century Nagarakrtagama chronicle of Majapahit regarding an inaugural ritual in which a priest symbolically separates and opens the fringe of a continuous-warp fabric (*pegat sigi*).

A similar ritual of separating the warp is performed today in two former Majapahit centers in Lombok—Sembalun and Bayan—where priests use striped cotton cloths with a continuous warp that look, on first glance, remarkably like the Balinese *wangsul*. This sacred *kombong umbak* ritual is performed as part of rites of passage and in festivals celebrated at sacred springs. The names of mythological persons and sacred weapons invoked are Hindu-Javanese in derivation, indicating that Javanese princes probably once lived here as generals and governors, and that sacred textiles with continuous warps were then used in rituals from

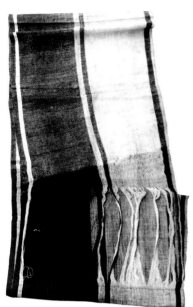

which the present ones derive. In the rituals now performed by village Sasak priests in these two villages, such cloths continue to play a central role, as the closed warp threads are cut and opened, thus symbolizing the liberation of previously bound forces.

Yarn and cloth are widely believed in Indonesia to be replete with beneficial powers to ward off harm or protect against misfortune. In a general sense they also represent a powerful binding and connecting element or bonding force. In rituals performed in Bali today, the transcendental forces embodied in cotton yarns are also symbolically liberated through a ritual cutting of the warp threads (*pegatin sandangan*), wholly or partially, by a priest or priestess. The force stored in the continuous warps is thereby released.

This symbolic liberation of bound energies comes very clearly to the fore in the Balinese hair-cutting ritual performed 210 days after the birth of a child. During this ceremony, the infant is permitted to touch the earth with its feet for the first time—described as a "return" to earth (*wangsul*) in which it is transformed from a divine being into a human. Such symbolism is also clearly present in death ceremonies through which the soul is released from the material body. In various parts of Bali, when a village or temple priest (*pemangku*) dies, a *ngelad pemangku* ceremony is performed in which a pure white *wangsul* cloth is first hung up at the altar (*sanggah tutuan*) and then cut. The deceased is thereby symbolically released from his earthly tasks (*ngayah di pura*), at the same time that the bond between him and his temple association is severed.

The ritual usage of *wangsul* is dwindling in many areas, or has even died

Figure 5.5 (left): *Atu-atu* cloth. Cotton. South Bali. 136 x 50 cm. MEB IIc 20332.

Figure 5.6 (above): *Wangsul/gedogan raina wengi* ("day/night"). The cloth expresses symbolically the dualism of day and night as well as the alternation of light and dark (*seliwah*). Private collection, Karangasem.

out altogether. In Badung, Tabanan and Bangli, other yellow and white materials or golden *perada* and *songkèt* cloths have taken their place. However, entire collections of more or less ancient *wangsul* are still to be found in Klungkung, Karangasem and Bulèlèng, where they have been carefully preserved by women of priestly rank specializing in the lore of sacrificial offerings. These cloths are used in rituals, and are sometimes even loaned out for use by others. But even here, in the more conservative areas of Bali, simple white sashes or rings are increasingly being used as cheap substitutes for cloths woven from locally grown cotton and dyed using natural colors.

Only in a few Brahmanic compounds (*gria*) do people still take the time to produce elaborate striped *wangsul* cloths for major rituals. For this purpose, the weavers use the same horizontal *cagcag* looms on which *songkèt* is produced, but without the reed (since a circular warp is being woven). The old horizontal backstrap loom without a reed is also still in use in Tenganan for weaving double *ikats* and striped *anteng gedogan*, and may still be found in Lombok as well, but there are few traces of it outside these areas.

SACRED CLOTH IN RITES OF PASSAGE

Balinese sacrificial rituals in which a central place is accorded to humans can be divided into two groups: the *manusa yadnya* and *pitra yadnya* mentioned above. The former begins with marriage and procreation and continues through various stages of child-raising, serving during pregnancy to strengthen the embryo in the mother's womb, and during and after birth to ensure the safety of mother and child. It is then concerned with various phases of life until, on reaching adulthood, a person marries and founds his or her own family. These ceremonies are all organized privately by the parents. The second group of transitional rituals comprises the death ceremony and an elaborate sequence of other rites, all of which must be performed by children for their parents.

In south and southwest Bali, especially in places where magic, soothsaying and trance figure prominently, the parents of a newborn child pay a visit to a medium (*balian taksu*) several days after its birth. The medium establishes contact with the ancestors and learns whose soul has been reincarnated in the infant's body. The reincarnated ancestor can, when asked, then express preferences concerning the performance of rites to be held and the accoutrements to be used, including the *bebali* cloths in which the child must be clad on the occasion of the three-month ritual, or the ritual held after six Balinese months (210 days).

Such rituals serve the well-being of the child in body and spirit. They also pay honor to his four symbolic older brothers and sisters (*catur sanak* or *kanda mpat*), who enable the embryo to survive in the womb, who then accompany the birth and who, provided they are well treated, will accompany the person beyond death. The *kanda mpat*—amniotic fluid (*yeh nyom*), vernix caseosa (*lamas*), blood (*getih*) and placenta (*ari-ari*)—are of vital importance once the child has assumed human shape in the womb. In the fulfillment of their protective tasks, they are supported by a total of 108 forces (*bajang*), which begin by functioning as useful assistants; after birth, however, they turn into troublemakers and have to be removed by ritual means. The exorcism of the *bajang*, whose survival might endanger the further development of the child, is part of a colorful

Figure 5.7: Prior to the puberty and tooth-filing rituals the *bebali* cloths are piled up and ritually purified with incense (red cloths are called *sekordi barak*, black ones *kulangsih*). Karangasem.

ritual held either during the three-month festival, or on the first birthday held after six months according to the Hindu-Javanese calendar. The latter is know as an *otonin*, and at this time the child and its four symbolic siblings enter a new phase of existence, coming into contact for the first time with the powers of nature. They are given new names and are brought before the *pedanda*, the Brahman priest—and hence simultaneously before the god Siwa—for purification and dedication.

In this important and dangerous transition from one stage of life to the next, *wangsul* and *bebali* cloths play their first and indispensable role in the ritual proceedings. This will be described here in the form in which they typically appear during the six-month festival (*otonin*), parts or elements of which also appear in the three-month festival. The form and content of the ritual, especially as regards the use of certain sacred cloths, is similar throughout Bali, though there are many differences of detail depending, as the Balinese are fond of saying, on the "village, time and social pattern" (*désa, kala, patera*).

THE 210-DAY BIRTHDAY RITUAL

After 210 days, a child is thought to be no longer a manifestation of God, but an earthly being in need of protection. Having previously been carried everywhere by parents and siblings, it experiences its initial contact with Mother Earth, touching the earth (*ngenteg Pertiwi*) with its feet for the first time at the family's altar of origin, the *sanggah kamulan*. This takes place at the beginning of the *moton*, early in the morning before the sun has risen. In various parts of Bali it is customary to clothe the child in a protective *bebali* hip cloth for this important occasion.

Figure 5.8: The candidates of the tooth-filing ceremony are covered with green and red checked *bebali* cloths (*selulut*). The head is placed on a cushion wrapped with a striped *ules galeng*. Karangasem, Sidemen.

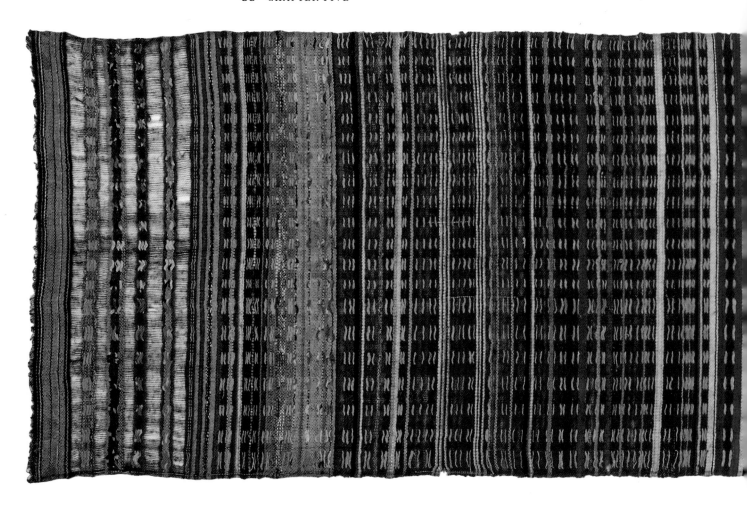

Figure 5.9: *Kakancan. Bebali* cloth for rites of passage. Cotton, hand spun. In some of the stripes supplementary wefts and parts made according to à jour technique. South Bali. 158 x 44 cm. MEB IIc 16997.

This morning ceremony takes place quietly in the house temple, in the bosom of the family. The ritual purification and votive acts which follow in the afternoon are an elaborate and more public celebration, however. As a rule, a Brahman priest or priestess is invited to conduct the rite, before a large gathering of relatives, friends and neighbors. As the priest dons his vestments and purifies himself with water, work goes on around him to make ready the utensils for making holy water, and to prepare the accoutrements and meal offerings intended for the deity to whom the ritual is addressed, along with the sacred cloths appointed for the occasion.

In the first phase of the ritual, the disturbing *bajang* forces from the child's surroundings are banished, after some of the impurities still adhering to the child following its emergence from the womb have first been transferred to them. In the scene set for this ritual, which is organized by the women, the place of the child is temporarily taken by a pumpkin (*beligo*, Fig. 5.10), a banana blossom (*pusuh*), or sometimes by a cucumber (*ketimun*), which thus substitutes for the child as a changeling. The *bajang* are represented in the ceremony in the form of a duck's egg (*taluh*), a black stone (*batu bulitan*) and a coconut-palm spathe with anthropomorphic chalk drawings (*papah*).

The objects and offerings set aside for this elaborate deception and subsequent exorcism of the *bajang* are placed on a long wooden bench in the open central courtyard, in between two pavilions. In the middle of the bench is placed a plaited basket with the *bajang* symbols, a used earthenware pot, a conical plaited container for steaming rice, and several small plaited packets containing rice paste. Near the basket is placed a silver dish with *wangsul* and *bebali* cloths, which must also undergo ritual purification before they can be used. At the outer end of the bench is a small stone mortar with a pestle containing a handful of unhusked rice grains—symbols of well-being and fertility— and a viaticum for the *bajang*.

In one of the pavilions the priest busies himself with the preparation of holy water, while in the other are placed food offerings for the god and for the child. Ritual objects required for a circular procession by the household women—the *milehan bajang*—are placed in the middle of the compound, ready for a ritual purification with holy water, which is then sprinkled all around the ritual space by means of a whisk made of artistically cut young coconut-palm leaves (*lis*).

Upon completion of the purification ritual, the changeling (a pumpkin in many parts of Bali, a banana blossom in the north) is decorated to represent the child—with fontanelle plate, arms, legs and finger rings. It is then perfumed and finally clothed with one or more *wangsul* or *bebali*. In Karangasem, people use multicolored cloths with an undivided fringe and a striped pattern, the apparent "center" of which proves, upon closer examination, to be slightly offset to one side and therefore asymmetrical (Fig. 5.1). In the Balinese principle of dualism, right and left are always unequal in size (*ibah*). Any excess in the left, or feminine, part is thought to create life (*pangurip*). Power or energy (*taksu*) can only develop from the two asymmetrical parts mutually completing each other.

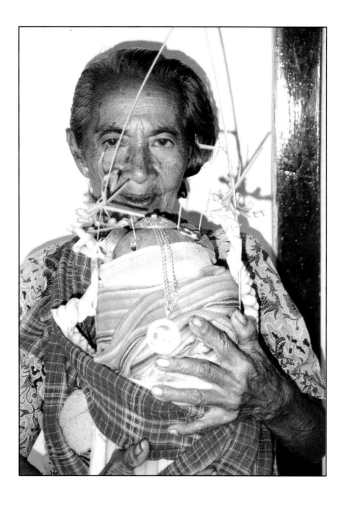

The ceremony which follows is performed twice, once for the changeling and again for the real child. It usually begins with a ritual bath in purifying holy water (*tirta palukatan*) in a flat earthenware dish (*paso, pané*). Wherever possible, the dish is set on the top of a large stone rice mortar (*lesung*). A *wangsul/gedogan* is placed in the earthenware vessel as a liner (*tatakan*), the cloth chosen being an *atu-atu*—a fabric with regular white and dark blue stripes, or groups of two and three blue stripes arranged on both sides of a broad blue stripe set, again, in the apparent center.

The *bajang* procession now proceeds three times clockwise and three times counterclockwise around the offerings and place of ablution, led by a tall leafy bamboo branch (*penjor*) and shaded by a broadly spreading *kumbang* leaf used as a ceremonial parasol. A woman in the procession carries the pumpkin, symbolically stamping on grains of rice at each round, as the mother also does with the real child later. The act of stamping symbolically highlights the importance of growth and fertility.

Immediately after this procession, the changeling is carried before the priest, who handles it, purifies it, and sprinkles it with holy water just as if it were the real child. Finally it goes back to the *bajang* offerings, where the women at first use their hands to waft the essence of the sacrifices toward it (*natabin*). It is then placed in a carrier fashioned of plaited coconut-palm leaves and lovingly rocked to and fro to the strains of a

Figure 5.10: The changeling *bajang beligo*, taking the place of the child temporarily during the three or six month festivals, is decorated and wrapped in *wangsul/gedogan* cloths. For carrying the changeling a *selulut* cloth is being used. Karangasem, Sidemen.

lullaby. Finally the pumpkin is denuded without further ado, carried out of the house along with the *bajang* offerings, and discarded at the nearest road crossing.

After the air has been thus purified and the disturbing *bajang* forces have left the site, the real child moves into the focus of priestly rituals of lustration and dedication. In preparation for its first great appearance before the priest and God, it is adorned and clad in a *bebali* cloth (Figs. 5.9, 5.11). In the former kingdom of Bulèlèng in north Bali, which like most of the former kingdoms is identical with the present *kabupaten* (administrative district), the child wears a *kakancan* cloth for the subsequent ceremonies of *natab* (reception of the essence of the offerings) and *matirta* (reception of holy water), and for the concluding hair-cutting ritual (*mapetik*) and prayer (*mabakti*). Here, *tulang mimi*, *salang waluh* or *surya candra* cloths are customarily used. Common to all these cloths is the color of the banana blossom—red or reddish blue—and contrary to the practice in other areas like Karangasem, these *bebali* are worn first by the changeling (*pusuh*) and then by the child. (In Karangasem, on the other hand, the child's clothing is fetched only when the pumpkin changeling, laden with impurities, has been thrown away.) For the ritual bath (*magogogogoan*), or immediately following it, the baby is then clad in the first *bebali* of its life and is then brought before the priest. In noble families in east Bali, preference is still given to the red *sekordi* (*sekordi barak*), an open weave with a red background and a white, yellow, or orange-checkered pattern.

However, before the baby is ready for the priestly ceremony, it must be divested of other impure elements. For this reason, after three perambulations around the rice mortar (*milehan lesung*), the child is first brought to the flat earthenware dish filled with purifying water (*palukatan*). The container is like a pool (*taman*) of life, in which float those things or characteristics which are important for later existence: an inscribed *lontar* leaf betokening intelligence or wisdom; Chinese coins representing wealth (but also an addiction to gambling); grains of rice or maize for industriousness and diligence; golden and silver rings expressing a need for ornamentation or vanity. Various river creatures—small fish, cray-

Figure 5.11: The baby is dressed with a *kakancan bebali* hip cloth on the occasion of the three-month festival (*nelubulanin*, high Balinese *nigang sasihin*). Karangasem.

fish, or eels—bring life to the symbolic pool, from which the infant fishes out with his right hand those things which he will have in abundance during his lifetime. During this *magogo-gogoan* ceremony, a loosely plaited cock basket (*guungan*) is placed like a protective roof over the child, who is then purified with water splashed from the earthenware container. Finally, the last impurities are picked from the fontanelle by a chicken (*mapacokin siap*). Only then can the important hair-cutting ritual be performed by the priest.

It is the purpose of all *manusa yadnya* to release the growing person in several stages from blemishes, sins, and temptations, and it is at this point that a further set of elements felt to be impure or dirty (referred to collectively as *mala*) are removed. In a symbolic act, the meaning of which is clear even to strangers, the priest uses a large pair of scissors to cut five locks of hair from the infant's head in the cardinal directions ruled by the most important gods and demons—to the side of the sunrise and sunset, to the mountains and the sea, and in the center. Together with pierced Chinese coins, betel leaves and sometimes a few threads from the fringed edge of a *wangsul/gedogan* cloth, the hairs are put into a long conically rolled coconut-palm leaf (*belayag*) and carefully laid on a *wangsul/gedogan* placed in a silver dish.

Among the striped cloths which might be used, preference is given to those which, because of their nine colors, can be identified with the ninefold system of divine classification (*nawasanga*) symbolized by the lotus blossom (*padma*) or by the weapon attributes of the nine deities which command the eight directions and the center. The nine-striped *perémbon* cloth is therefore called a *perémbon nawasanga* by Brahmans. In spite of its many colors, the cloth is felt in this case to be a totality and a symbol of unity in which each stripe represents a whole *bebali* cloth (*sekordi* or *selulut*, for example) or a whole *wangsul/gedogan* (such as a *pageh tuuh* or *nagasari*).

Where no continuous-warp striped cloths are available, a number of small, square cloths known as *kakasang* are used to place the hair upon. It is interesting to note that they are also combined with *nawasanga*,

Figure 5.12: *Wangsul/gedogan raina wengi* ("day/night"). Part of the *jajanganan* offering which is prepared on the occasion of the rites of passage ritual, 105 or 210 days after birth. Karangasem.

which in this instance are represented with embroidered lotus blossoms or weapons. Depending on the priest's views in the matter, the hair is buried near the altar of origin and hence returned to the earth mother Pertiwi, or thrown into a nearby body of water, either the sea or a river.

Among the votive offerings used during the first rites of passage—especially those performed 105 and 210 days after birth—there is one of particular importance. It is called *jajanganan* ("all kinds of vegetables") and consists of a flat container, like a large rice-winnowing fan, in which fruits, vegetables and cakes are piled over uncooked rice, coins and a strand of white cotton yarn. To this offering a folded black-and-white cloth (Figs. 5.6, 5.12) in the form of a *raina wengi* ("day-night") or *seliwah* ("between light and dark") are added as a vestment (*wastra*), or else as an "accompaniment" (*dedampingan*). These symbolically express the dualism of day and night, or the alternation of light and dark, which the child now experiences consciously, and which will permanently shape his future life. The custom of placing folded *gedogan/wangsul* as an "accompaniment" to the offerings, or alternatively of covering them with such cloths, still survives, most notably in east Bali. As liners (*tatakan*) which separate the sacred gift from the profane, *wangsul/gedogan* are still used today throughout Bali.

MEETING THE GODS OF LOVE

In studying Balinese religion, the methods of participative observation and interrogation are satisfactory only up to a certain point. For all important questions of religious theory, history, medicine and law, consultation of written sources—*lontar* palm-leaf manuscripts inscribed with sharp-pointed knives—must be consulted, just as local ritual specialists do when they need to know more about a particular ritual. Balinese rituals are based, on the one hand, on oral traditions shaped by local developments; this is the source of their colorfulness and distinctiveness, as well as of the local variations found from one place to another. On the other hand, the authoritative *lontar* documents consulted by Brahmans tend to impose a certain uniformity. Whereas these *lontar* have little to say about rites of passage concerning infants, they give more detailed recommendations on the use of sacred textiles in puberty ceremonies, tooth filings, weddings and the like.

Figure 5.13: *Wangsul/gedogan usap rai.* White cotton cloth with uncut warp. Semara and Ratih as deities of love, below a lotus symbol. Private collection, Karangasem.

In the written sources a clear distinction is made between cloths worn as part of the ritual dress during a *natab* ceremony (the reception of the essence of offerings), and those which are used as liners (*tatakan wangsul*) to separate the sacred from the profane. According to the texts, an underskirt cloth *padang derman* (named after a kind of grass) should be worn by women during this part of the ritual. It is made of two widths of woven cotton and has a red or dark green background with stripes of various shades. In addition to *padang derman*, it is also possible to wear *cepuk* as an inner hip cloth (see Chapter 8). The most important hip cloths (*kamben, wastra*) for both sexes are *sekordi barak* (Fig. 5.3) and *sekordi gadang* (red and green *sekordi*, a name which derives from *suka wredhi*, meaning "happiness and fertility") with delicate white or yellow checked patterns, and *kulangsih*—a black cloth with a white or light blue checked pattern. Red and green *sekordi* (the latter are also called *sia laki*) are still frequently seen in Bulèlèng and Karangasem; *kulangsih* are worn in Karangasem, mostly by members of the old Balinese *sudra* or *jaba* commoner clans. Both sexes wear a multicolored striped *wangsul/gedogan bagus anom* (meaning "pretty and young") as a sash band (*sabuk, pakekek*).

At maturation ceremonies (*menék kelih, rajasvala*) and tooth-filing rituals (*matatah, mapandes*) the preferred cloths for outer wraparound (*saput, kampuh*) are *geringsing, prabhu, kayu sugih, suddhamala* or *selulut*. Particularly in east Bali, where yellow breast cloths have become common, candidates in the tooth-filing ceremony are still covered up to the breast with a *selulut* (meaning "united in love"), a cloth with a green background and small squares of light green and large ones of red, which affords protection against the dangers of transition into a new life (Fig. 5.8). The purpose of tooth filings, where the six upper canine and incisor teeth are filed down, is to reduce to a reasonable level the following six human passions: 1. *kama* (lust, sensual love); 2. *krodha* (rage, anger); 3. *loba* (covetousness); 4. *moha* (confusion, stupidity); 5. *mada* (frenzy due to passion or drunkenness), and 6. *matsarya* (jealousy, envy).

The candidate lies prone on a mattress covered with a plaited mat on which the gods of love, Semara and Ratih, are depicted. The head is placed on a cushion covered with a blue-white striped *atu-atu* cloth (Fig. 5.5) or a *kemit* with gray lozenges, or with yellow-white squares (*pelangka gading*). Anyone possessing a *geringsing* or *wangsul* also wraps this around the cushion (Fig. 9.11). Cushions with these patterns are piled in odd numbers (5, 7, 9, 11) near the offerings (*galeng tumpuk*) and express the social status or the caste of the family. Gags (*pedangal*), together with spittoons made out of young, yellow coconuts, are placed on a bed of *wangsul* cloths nearby. Pieces of sugarcane or wood from the magical *dapdap* tree are placed behind the back molars to prop open the mouth during the filing, and the tooth-filing specialist (*sangging*), usually a Brahman, then takes up his hammer, chisel and file.

Semara and Ratih, who figure prominently in all later maturation ceremonies, are given their own place of sacrifice, being represented in a close embrace on cloths and mats in the style of Balinese *wayang* figures. Actual initiation rites are always preceded by a period of three days' seclusion (*ngekeb*) in which the male and female principles represented by these gods meet (*mapedamel*). The candidates first receive food, spices and drinks from the hand of their mothers in the six basic tastes—sweet, sour, salty, tangy, bitter, and burning hot (*sadrasa*)—and thus learn, in a

Figure 5.14: During the seclusion prior to tooth filing the candidates stroke forehead and cheek with cloth displaying the design of the gods of love, Semara and Ratih, and thus become involved in a symbolic manner with love. Karangasem.

figurative sense, to know the true measure of all things. Finally they take the fringed part of an undyed *wangsul* cloth decorated with a depiction of the love gods between the thumb and index finger, and let Semara and Ratih slip gently over their cheek (*ngusap rai, ngares pipi*). (Figs. 5.13, 5.14).

CLOTHING FOR HUMANS, ANCESTORS AND ALTARS

Since relations with the gods mirror those on earth, the same attitude is adopted toward deities as toward very highly placed members of society. With reverent gestures, they are offered everything considered to be of great value: raw and cooked foods, drinks and betel chews, ornaments and, of course, folded cloths piled one atop the other, tied with a strip of tape and set in a place of sacrifice as divine apparel (*tigasan, rantasan*).

When the great Balinese clan temples celebrate their anniversaries, and when buildings are consecrated after being completed or restored (*ngenteg linggih*), it is the custom to place three parcels of four to five unused *bebali* and *wangsul* cloths before the three compartments of the ancestral shrine (*ibu, pajenengan*), which correspond in composition to sets of human clothing, viz. inner hip cloth, hip cloth, outer hip cloth, sash and breast cloth.

As determined by the cardinal points, the cloths on the mountain side are black, green or blue (e.g. *kulangsih, uyah areng, sia laki*); in the center they are multicolored (e.g. *kayu tulak, perémbon, alang-alang segabung*); and on the seaward side they are red (e.g. *sekordi barak, urab kecicang*). In the family temple of the Buddhist priests and priestesses of Budakeling in east Bali, there are three mutually independent altars resembling human beings clad from head to foot in *bebali* cloths and *wangsul/gedogan*. The Balinese concept according to which everything is divisible into three component areas, or zones (*tri hita karana*) has led to a hierarchical tripartition of the upper world, middle world and lower world being applied to human beings and almost everything else that has a head, trunk and foot. This includes the house and its component parts, as well as the shrines and altars in temples, which are divided into a foot, body and head and dressed like human beings in order to provide them with protection (Fig. 5.4a-c).

—*U. Ramseyer*

CHAPTER SIX

Keling

Archaic Cloths from Nusa Penida

WHEN Indonesian President Suharto and his wife paid an official visit to the island of Nusa Penida in May of 1983, schoolboys in the main town of Batununggul welcomed the distinguished guests with a traditional *baris* dance. A reporter from the *Bali Post* newspaper noted with some surprise that the dancers were not wearing gold-bespangled *perada* cloths, as would have been the custom in Bali, but typical archaic Nusa Penida fabrics: striped *keling* inner hip cloths, with outer hip cloths or *saput* made of *cepuk* (see Chapter 8). This expression of the care devoted to the preservation of the local cultural heritage won words of praise from the visitors.

As in east Bali, striped and checked textiles used in connection with festive ceremonies and rituals belong to a category known as *gedogan* (see Chapter 5). Most of these fabrics have multicolored stripes in the warp, others have small checks, and both are generally referred to in Nusa Penida as *keling*. These were formerly made exclusively from handspun local cotton, but are also woven today from industrially spun yarns.

In both Balinese and Indonesian, the word *keling* refers to an "Indian" or "Indian merchant" (after the name of the ancient South Indian kingdom of Kalinga), and its use here may thus indicate that such textiles, or possibly the colors used to make them, were originally imported by Indian or Arab merchants. The roots of this term, however, may be older; it may be related to Tenganan myths concerning the primal ancestors of this old Balinese village—the wife Keling and her husband Kaung. The latter supposition is supported by the fact that *keling* cloths still have definite female connotations, and traditionally should not be worn by men.

In earlier times, homemade *keling* underskirts or breast cloths formed the most distinctive part of the everyday garb of Nusa Penida women. The climate and geology of this barren island is similar to that of the dry Bukit peninsula in south Bali, and both places lent themselves well to cotton cultivation. Elderly women formerly cleaned, carded and spun the fibers into rather coarse yarns, a small portion of which were then sold abroad—to Tenganan, among other places, where they were used in the manufacture of *geringsing* cloths. Dyeing was done with the same vegetable dyes used for *cepuk* cloths (see Chapter 8), and during the 1930s almost every house compound in the central plateau villages of Nusa Penida had one or two clattering *cagcag* looms on which girls and

Figure 6.1 (opposite and above): *Keling* cloth. Cotton. Nusa Penida. 276 x 55 cm. MEB IIc 20409.

young women wove *keling*. Even in the early 1960s there were between 100 and 200 looms in the villages of Sekartaji, Pelilit and Tanglad, and more than 200 in Sakti, Karang and Karangsari.

In those days, women wore the long *tapih keling* as an everyday inner hip cloth under a shorter dark blue or black outer hip cloth, thus showing the colored stripes at the bottom to advantage. By the 1920s, however, Javanese batik and cheap, gaudy manufactured cloths of European origin had begun to make their appearance in markets on the north coast of the island, and these rapidly displaced the locally-produced products. Following Indonesian independence, these imported fabrics gained increasing acceptance, spreading even to the most remote villages in the highlands, and cotton cultivation steadily declined in this period. But *keling* cloths have not disappeared altogether from Nusa Penida—they are still woven by a few elderly women for their own needs, as well as being produced for sale because of their important ritual uses. Today they are worn by women of the older generation only, or only for very special occasions. As such, they are evidence of an earlier and more pristine period in the history of this remote and conservative island, maintaining an identification with the "real" Nusa Penida.

RITUAL USES OF KELING CLOTHS

At an *otonin* (6-month birthday) festival in a *ksatria* family in Batunung-gul, the child's mother exchanges her breast cloth of colored terry for a breast cloth made of *keling kacang ijo* ("mung bean *keling*") which is checked with red, yellow, white and black squares. This is done during the last part of the ritual when, together with her husband, she receives a final purification from the priestess in the form of a sprinkling of holy water. At another birthday festival, *keling* cloths serve as symbolic clothing for a banana blossom placed on a silver dish and made up to represent a "changeling" or deceptive substitute for the child (see Chapter 5). The blossom is tightly wrapped with strands of handspun cotton (Fig. 6.2), and underneath it are placed a carefully folded red-and-yellow checked *keling* and a *seléndang gedogan* (see below).

In an east coast village, a *balik sumpah* ceremony—a high *bhuta yadnya* ritual to chase away unfavorable spirits—is celebrated in a family compound. The columns of the central rice barn (*jineng*) are completely enveloped in *keling*, while others are spread out under the great roof as symbolic protection for the offerings piled up below. Similar protective functions are performed by fabrics used in a special *bayuh* ritual held for

Figure 6.2 (left): Changeling with adornment, *benang Bali* and clothes of *keling* and *seléndang gedogan* at a six-month ceremony (*otonin*). Nusa Penida.

Figure 6.3 (right): Weaving a *seléndang gedogan*. Nusa Penida.

a young man in a remote mountain village, who had the misfortune to be born in an unpropitious week. He was therefore thought to be at particular risk to bedevilment by spirits, and had in fact been seriously ill on several occasions. An *asegan*—a temporary construction made of bamboo and draped over and over with finely-checked *keling* with white or black backgrounds—was erected for his ritual purification by holy water. In a similar way, checked and striped *keling* cloths, including some extremely rare forms with broader stripes, are used to convert the temporary site for the body of a deceased person into a purified place. When used as wall hangings and canopies such fabrics afford protection from evil influences.

A particularly impressive manifestation of the power of *keling* cloths is to be seen in their use in cloth offerings (*rantasan*), when they acquire the status of appropriate presents to gods and divine ancestors. When the

Figure 6.4 (left): Textile offering (*rantasan*) with knife at a *menék daha* ritual.

Figure 6.5 (above): Young girl with holy-water vessel in *seléndang gedogan* in a procession before the cremation of a village priest. Nusa Penida.

menék daha ceremony (rite of passage at puberty) is performed for the little daughter of a village chief, a tiny plaited basket, barely noticeable, is found among the profusion of sacrificial offerings. A knife, associated with the important concept of "opening the right way," is placed in the basket together with a bundle of very old striped and checked *gedogan* fabrics on top of a folded *keling* cloth which is dark indigo blue with fine, white checked stripes (Fig. 6.4). Later the *pemangku*, a simple village priest, explains that this *rantasan* may only contain fabrics employing vegetable dyes, and that at least four colors must be represented—white, yellow, red and blue (black)—but that ideally eight should be used. These colors symbolize the four points of the compass and the divine powers associated with them, combined in the center in a multicolored pattern for the god Siwa.

A few days later the wife of this priest, an experienced specialist in sacrificial offerings (*tukang banten*), puts together a giant textile offering (*pajegan*) for a wedding composed of her own and borrowed cloths (Fig. 1.9). No fewer than 24 folded fabrics are piled one on top of the other to form a high tower fixed with bamboo poles and *benang Bali* ("handspun Balinese thread"), and draped and bound together with modern textiles. All of the folded fabrics in the pile are traditional cloths from Nusa Penida: monochrome rust-red, dark green and black fabrics, along with coarse locally produced *endek*, checked and fine or broad-striped *keling*, and on top a *cepuk*. The whole construction is crowned with a headcloth (*destar*) that marks it as a male *pajegan*.

For weddings of a higher grade, a pair of such *pajegan* is used, one male and one female, while for a lower-grade ceremony three cloths in a single pile will suffice. The sequence of cloths in the pile is immaterial, but there must be eight colors and their combination—so that here again we find a reference to the link with divine powers and their corresponding compass directions. In principle all the cloths should be of handspun cotton to symbolize the relationship of the community to the ancestors, and to the earth goddess Déwi Pertiwi who taught mankind how to grow and process cotton. With the exception of the *songkèt* headcloth and the modern outer wrappings, this condition is fulfilled in the *pajegan* described above.

Besides *keling*, another type of striped textiles is still found in Nusa Penida which belong to the category of ritual *gedogan* cloths. They have small geometric supplementary warp or weft patterns between vertical or horizontal stripes, and are simply referred to as *seléndang gedogan*. Old *seléndang gedogan* are treasured as precious family heirlooms. In comparison with *cepuk* cloths, new fabrics of this type are fairly expensive, as the fine raw material is not cheap and the weaving process with additional pattern heddle rods (Fig. 6.3) is exacting and time-consuming. They are used in birthday ceremonies to wrap up or carry the child and changeling, and in major processions as a cloth in which to bear important ritual objects such as silver vessels containing holy water (Fig. 6.5).

—*M.L. Nabholz-Kartaschoff*

CHAPTER SEVEN

Polèng

The Dualism of Black and White

W ITH their chessboard pattern of alternating black and white squares, running in an unending sequence to form long strips, *polèng* cloths are impossible to miss. Look for a long time at this striking pattern, and it engraves itself indelibly on the memory, and the oscillation between black and white, the most radical of all contrasts, begins to dance before the eyes. Every visitor to Bali—be his stay never so short—will come across these textiles. To enter a temple you must file past the stone guardians whose hands rest on their sword hilts, ready to repel by force of arms anyone with evil intentions. These stone sculptures usually wear a hip cloth of *polèng* (Fig. 7.2). The black-and-white checked material not only bears a special pattern—black-and-white squares are common enough in the textiles of many cultures—but also conveys a special message, intimating to every Balinese complexes of meaning and significance which he grasps on seeing these cloths even though their purport is rarely verbalized.

WOVEN, PRINTED AND PLAITED PATTERNING

Polèng cloths are not sumptuous—they do not have the look of aristocratic luxury which is inseparable from, say, *songkèt*, nor are they technically difficult to make, as is the case with supplementary weft *ikat* materials like *endek*, *cepuk* and the double *ikat geringsing*. So what is it that gives these cloths their special character? Actually it is the black-and-white squares that has given the cloth its name. Neither the material—whether cotton or man-made fibers—nor the method of patterning (whether woven with white and black yarn or simply printed on the finished white cloth) makes any difference to its significance and its functions. For all these cloths with a visually identical or similar appearance, the same expression is used: *polèng*.

However, between printed and woven *polèng*, there is a distinction that does not appear to matter very greatly to the local observer today: the woven cloth contains, in addition to pitch-black and snow-white squares, also squares that are gray in color. These are created when the varicolored yarns of warp and weft intersect one another; they are markedly less conspicuous than the pure black and white (Fig. 7.3).

It is no longer known with any certainty whether there were specialized localities and weaving centers which produced *polèng* almost exclusively

Figure 7.1 (opposite): *Polèng* (detail). Silk. Karangasem. 147 x 117 cm. MEB IIc 18796.

and then sold them all over the island. Many of the printed cloths now come from textile mills in Java. But there are still in Denpasar (and presumably elsewhere in Bali) home-weavers who regularly produce *polèng*.

If woven *polèng* fabrics (regarded as *kuna* or "ancient" in Bali and thought to be of local origin) are examined closely, the impression created is one of black and white bands that cross alternately as if interwoven. There are actually some very simple decorative scrolls of plant material, called *lamak*, whose pattern resembles *polèng*. They are made by simply stitching together a light-colored almost beige palm leaf and a dark green one. *Lamak* scrolls of this kind are often placed in the niche of those shrines which during temple festivals are almost entirely draped in *polèng* cloths, and allowed to hang down. To what extent the two patterns, plaited and woven or printed, are directly related—whether *polèng* on textiles has been modelled on an undoubtedly older plaiting pattern—cannot be determined with any certainty. We once saw another variant of the *polèng* pattern at Dalem Peed on Nusa Penida. There they used white cloths on which the black squares were painted by hand.

Incidentally, the black and white squares are not of equal size in all *polèng* patterns. There are textiles with small, medium and large checks and the width of the squares ranges from about one up to ten centimeters. Cloths with small and medium-sized checks often are combined, as for example, in the case of the stone seats in temples when these are decorated with *polèng* during annual festivals. Textiles with larger patterns are used for the hip cloth (*wastra*), while those with a small pattern for the cloth (*kampuh*) that is wrapped over it. The very largest checks I have always seen predominantly on the wraparounds of the giant masked figure of the Barong Landung (Fig. 7.5).

GUARDIANS, STONES AND TREES

The repertoire of uses to which *polèng* can be put is large. However, if all the types are viewed together, certain common features emerge in regard to significance. The stone temple guardians have already been

Figure 7.2 (above left): Guardian figure, standing on a small figure of a woman, in front of a shrine. To mark his readiness to take arms in self-defense he is wearing a *polèng* cloth. Sanur.

Figure 7.3 (above right): An abode of the gods draped with small check pattern and medium check pattern *polèng* cloths; palm-leaf *lamak* with *polèng* pattern hanging down in front of the offering niche. Sanur.

Figure 7.4 (opposite): Guardian statue in the form of a female demon before the entrance to the temple sanctuary. Sanur.

Figure 7.5: Barong Landung couple, shaded by black ceremonial parasols, on their way to the sea for a ritual purification ceremony. South Bali.

mentioned. They stand to the left and right of the entrance to the various types of temple, whether it be the temple of origin (*pura puseh*), the village temple (*pura désa*), or the chthonic or netherworld *pura dalem*. Other types of sanctuaries also have guardians in the form of demons with bulbous eyes and with bared teeth, often with long canine fangs and squat, muscular bodies. These are adorned with *polèng* wraparounds and sometimes headbands as well (Fig. 7.4). At Dalem Peed on Nusa Penida men are sometimes recruited as living guardians on certain occasions in the temple. They are clearly distinguished by their apparel. They wear a red headcloth and a black hip cloth with a long *polèng* cloth over it, from the back of which peeps the hilt of a *keris* (Fig. 7.9). I saw precisely the same combination of clothes, and especially the composition of colors (which have symbolic significance) in Bali displayed on stone sculptures guarding the entrance to a sea temple (*pura segara*).

A prominent feature of many sanctuaries is the *balé kulkul*, the tower-like construction at whose top hangs the slit-gong (*kulkul*), which is beaten to transmit signals. The body of the drum is often wrapped in a *polèng* cloth. Inside the temple some of the uses made of *polèng* display striking characteristics: in addition to guardian figures, also posted there in front of the principal shrines and likewise wearing *polèng*, there are also simple stone pillars and open stone seats (*tugu*) which have these textiles wrapped round their corpus. Sometimes, if these seats have a sacrificial niche closed on three sides as a "head," the tip is also adorned with a *polèng*, modeled on the men's headcloth, *destar*.

Only in rare cases are shrines, i.e. small closed wooden houses on a plinth with a central roof, decorated with *polèng* during temple festivals.

On the other hand, conspicuous and frequent use is made of them in small and medium-sized sanctuaries connected with the graveyard. This is exemplified by a *merajapati* located in a burial ground and consisting of a single shrine surrounded by a wall. Sometimes this structure is a so-called "temple of the dead." If the principal abode there is dedicated to the goddess Durga, then *polèng* are bound to be used.

In temple compounds consisting of several courtyards placed one behind the other—the innermost one being regarded as ritually the most sacred and pure—*polèng* will be used as a rule only in the first court. In the innermost part, white and yellow cloths normally predominate, while black-and-white checked cloths are seen there, if at all, on a stone pillar standing south of the most important shrines. This has to do with the cardinal points and their attributes. East and north are, in contrast to south and west, of innate pure qualities.

Polèng is never seen on shrines which have several superimposed pagoda-like *meru* roofs. The same holds true of the high open seat-type shrine, *padmasana*, which is connected with Siwa, Surya the sun, and also with the sacred Balinese mountain Gunung Agung. In the small open hall, which serves as a place for receiving the (invisible) gods as guests during festivals, *polèng* is not normally used.

Apart from temples that are walled off from outside, one very frequently encounters all over Bali, near the seashore or on the perimeter of a settlement, huge trees at the base of which is a small altar with numerous flower offerings and joss sticks. A *polèng* cloth is wound round the altar and sometimes round the tree trunk. The same applies to certain stones

Figure 7.6 (left): Abode of the central deity of Dalem Peed, Nusa Penida.

Figure 7.7 (right): Annual festival of a female deity whose symbol, a carved mask, is set up in front of her shrine. Its special function is marked by *polèng*. Sanur.

which are set up, usually near a tree, or leant inconspicuously against a temple wall as if by chance. Round them, too, a piece of *polèng* is wrapped (Fig. 1.10). Often only the "head" of the stone is visible. Except for an additional piece of white material, other textiles are rarely used there.

GODS OF THE NETHERWORLD

There are also temples in which almost all the seats are covered with this strikingly patterned cloth. The most impressive example (and also the most important in terms of significance) is the small temple near Dalem Peed on the island of Nusa Penida. It is a small sanctuary dedicated to the deity Ratu Gedé Mas Mecaling, measuring about 12 x 12 m. Within its confines grows a huge *waringin* (banyan) tree, its tangled roots embracing a stone column (made of single stones piled up) about 1.20 m. high. On its platform there is a stone head, humanoid in type but dis-

Figure 7.8: Shrine, adorned with *polèng*, honoring the deities of Dalem Peed in a sanctuary in south Bali.

playing the fangs, bulging eyes and distended nostrils typical of demons. This sculpture is almost completely covered with a *polèng* cloth. And there is *polèng* hanging from the column, on the top of which offerings are always laid out, and similar cloths wind around the *waringin* tree. This abode, dedicated to the forefathers of the god mentioned, also has a set of parasols which are covered with *polèng*; such parasols are always used as attributes of gods, deified ancestors, divine symbols and brahmanic priests. They are stuck in the ground near the stone altar (Fig. 7.6).

However, the most important feature of this sanctuary, which has been partly restored, is a shrine standing on a raised platform together with a small structure for offerings. It is at one and the same time a place for veneration and supplication. There the *pemangku*, the temple priest, accepts the offerings of the faithful and conducts the ritual. The shrine, which is again guarded by stone figures, is dedicated to Ratu Gedé Mas Mecaling. This part, the main precinct of the sanctuary, is also decorated almost exclusively with *polèng*, or, it would be no exaggeration to say, covered with a veritable skin of textiles. And here again we find *polèng* parasols which have the function and meaning of umbrella-shaped canopies. Many people make the pilgrimage to this temple, and those who have prayed and sacrificed there are given a *polèng* wristband as a token for their worship. The visual impact of this sanctuary, dressed overall with polèng is strong, provocative and yet somehow vaguely disturbing. In the southern region of the island of Bali itself there are those temples, dedicated wholly to Dalem Peed or possessing at least one important seat for Nusa Penida and the beings located there, which are characterized by the same liberal use of *polèng* (Fig. 7.8).

Polèng dominates the scene in another type of temple or parts thereof. These are the sanctuaries housing a pair of giant masked figures which are generally called Barong Landung. The Balinese speak of these figures, which are proxies for the corresponding divinities, as Ratu Gedé, the "Great Lord"; Barong Landung is a somewhat uncomplimentary name, which should not be uttered in their presence. It is to this couple that the central shrine of the sanctuary is invariably dedicated. The male figure is characterized by a giant body which, depending on the region, has a fur-like covering of hair or a "skin" of *polèng* material; his fearsome mien displays gleaming gold fangs. His wraparound consists of *polèng* with huge checks. By contrast his wife, who, according to written and oral tradition, is a Chinese woman who became the wife of a Balinese king, has a refined, bright and smiling face. Her apparel is sewn together from materials with different patterns that are accounted pleasing to the eye.

Ratu Gedé is a prodigious danger-averting figure who, on certain occasions, goes through the streets at night to drive away harm. But Ratu Gedé himself can also spread terror, for in certain places in south Bali he is also equated symbolically with Ratu Gedé Mas Mecaling, who, once a year at the beginning of the rainy season, lands with his horde of countless demons from Nusa Penida in south Bali, and from there spreads over the whole of Bali, bringing death and disease. On the night when the horde of the demon is expected and has to be mollified with offerings, the masked figure Ratu Gedé is borne through the streets of the village to ward off the evil threat. At the end of the rainy season, in spring, the deity returns to Nusa Penida with his retinue.

On another occasion, around the time of the Balinese New Year, Ratu

Figure 7.9: Traditional guardians clad in *polèng* at the sanctuary of Dalem Peed, Nusa Penida, on a ceremonial occasion.

Gedé is borne into a public village temple (with a central function) and placed there in the building for invisible gods and their material symbols (small anthropomorphic and zoomorphic wooden figures, flower symbols, and also masks and mask figures). By his side folded textiles are placed on an offering dish; these are cloth offerings dedicated to the god. These offerings, called *tigasan* or *rantasan* depending on the region and function, consist in the case of Ratu Gedé almost exclusively of *polèng* with checks of varying sizes.

Whereas the Barong Landung are the only anthropomorphic masked figures into which human beings can slip, there are other masks representing those symbols of divinities which are borne into the precincts of the temple during festivals (Fig. 7.7). And this is particularly the case with the *dalem* temples associated with graveyards. These are known as Rangda masks and are carried on cube-shaped baskets with lids into the temple on the heads of women. They are set up in small pavilions intended for them, usually to the south of the center in the innermost courtyard. In south Bali it is immediately evident on their entry which of the masks bears the name of a male and which of a female deity. A sash is wound in the manner of a belt round the plaited basket, which is generally used to keep the masks in. If the cloth is *polèng*, a male being is indicated, if white, a female one. Obviously nothing enables a further distinction to be made between the sexes either in the face or its attributes—wide-staring, bulging round eyes, a long tongue lolling from the mouth, and the lower canines jutting up far over the cheeks in the manner typical of other netherworld deities—nor in the way the hair is worn in a long reddish-brown, gray-streaked or white curly mane.

Whenever Rangda masks appear in the forecourt of a temple—and, as everyone knows, they do so as part of a fixed ritual performance—there will always be the zoomorphic masked figure of the Barong Kèt among them. Rangda and Barong stage a ritual fight or rather a contest of power between Rangda's destructiveness and Barong's benevolence. Among many other attributes, the apparel of the Rangda dancers includes *polèng* bands or breast cloths. Such fabrics are credited with inspiring the wearer with the fervor needed for the ritual dance and at the same time protecting him when Rangda is attacked by men in a trance (Fig. 7.10, 8.13).

During a temple festival, symbols of gods are carried into the precincts; this is usually done in the form of a procession which includes a gong orchestra. If the symbols refer primarily to netherworld deities, then one of the hand drums is wrapped in a *polèng* cloth, perhaps with a red border (Fig. 7.12). The figures of the deities and their attributes—cloth offerings, flower symbols, etc.—are accompanied by men who hold a parasol-like canopy over the sacred objects. The procession is headed by banners and flags. If they are made of *polèng*, this again relates directly to the netherworld gods and their symbols. On arrival at the temple, these

Figure 7.10: Appearance of Rangda in Sakenan during an annual festival. Her textile array consists of *polèng* and *cepuk* as well as a banner with a drawing of a demonic figure and a *polèng* pattern.

banners, flags and parasols are stuck in the ground in front of the seats of the deities. Such movable textile elements give the decorated sanctuary a more immediate and current significance. They underline the symbolism and meaning of the textiles used. *Polèng* has an unequivocal reference: to the gods of the netherworld.

BADGES FOR HUMAN BEINGS

The various fields we have described in which these black-and-white checked cloths are used will have given some idea of how *polèng* is involved in the context of religion and how it indicates the special spheres and their nature to which the gods belong. And now, when these conspicuously checked cloths are used not only for sacred stones, trees, shrines and divine symbols but are also worn by human beings (apart from Rangda dancers), their deeper significance and symbolic con-

Figure 7.11 (left): *Ogoh-ogoh* figure which is borne through the streets on the night before New Year to drive out demons and is then burnt. Sanur.

Figure 7.12 (above): Hand drum wrapped in *polèng* and red cloth. Tenganan.

tent begin to emerge more clearly. In Bali there is a category of dances known as *baris*, in which men, often divided into two groups and armed with long staves and spears, perform a ritual battle. *Baris* is often associated with trance—gods descend into the men and take possession of them. *Baris* is therefore a sacred dance. There is one village in south Bali which is known for a special kind of *baris* performed without any element of trance. The formation, which has been in existence from time immemorial, is called *baris polèng* (Fig. 7.13). It is always accompanied by its own gong orchestra. If invited, it will perform in other villages throughout the south Bali region.

As the name itself intimates, the dancers' apparel consists predominantly of *polèng*. They wear conical headdresses of this material with white "wings" at the sides. Small-checked *polèng* bands are wound round the chest and over the shoulders. There is actually a *polèng* belt and a *polèng* wraparound to go over black-and-white striped trousers. Over their shoulders the dancers wear a *geringsing* cloth (today sometimes replaced by an *ikat* cloth of the same colors from other east Indonesian islands). As the dance proceeds, these flap about like wings.

Baris polèng are invited into the villages of south Bali when a major cremation ceremony is to be performed for a deceased member of a high-born family. Today this is probably the most common occasion for its public appearance, though there may be other rites of passage (see Chapter 5) which make its presence desirable. The movements of the dancers are stately and majestic when they appear for the first time in front of the house compound. They wield their black-and-white striped spears (*tombak polèng*) as if to clear invisible obstacles out of the way, and as if they wanted to spread their pinions to fly up to the very sky.

Immediately following their performance—I was able to witness one performed at a cremation ceremony for a deceased Brahman priest in Sanur—the corpse was brought out of the compound and placed on the tower-like sedan chair. Dozens of men raised the chair bearing the mortal remains from the ground and carried them—part of the way in a wild gallop—to the cremation ground. There the body was bestowed in a sarcophagus shaped like a white bull decorated with gold paper. The life-size animal statue was then closed and set on fire in the cremation pavilion. As the first flames licked upwards, the *baris polèng* suddenly issued from behind nearby bushes. The group danced to the north of the cremation bull; the faces of the men were turned towards the cremation ground. Once again, accompanied by the gong orchestra, they slowly executed their steps, wielding their spears and lifting their arms, with *geringsing* cloths spreading above them like wings. As the flames took possession of the bull, the *baris polèng* disappeared again. Its task was completed. *Baris polèng* is conceived to be the escort of the soul that has quitted the body. *Baris polèng* prepares the way so that the soul can go to heaven without trouble; it combats demons and foes and helps the spirit

Figure 7.13: *Baris polèng,* on the occasion of a cremation ceremony for a brahman priest. South Bali.

to rise up into the firmament. *Polèng* has for this dance formation the same kind of significance as for the guardian figures in the temple: those wearing the cloth exercise a protective function.

Occasionally men can be seen wearing *polèng* at certain festivities. If you ask anyone why they have chosen this black-and-white checked cloth, the answer is usually brief and to the point: "Because he or she likes it." However, *polèng* is not used for every type of clothing. Men wear this material as a *kampuh*, a cloth worn over their hip cloth, or else as a sash, sometimes combined with a similarly patterned headcloth. As for the women, I actually saw only *polèng* sashes or a broad *polèng* cloth wrapped around waist and hips, but never, say, a *kebaya* blouse. The great majority of the men, and the women almost without exception, were not ordinary festival attenders but priests (*pemangku*) (Fig. 7.14) or men and women who had been elected by deities to be their epiphanies

Figure 7.14: Ritual at Dalem Peed, Nusa Penida. The *pemangku* steps along a path laid with *polèng*.

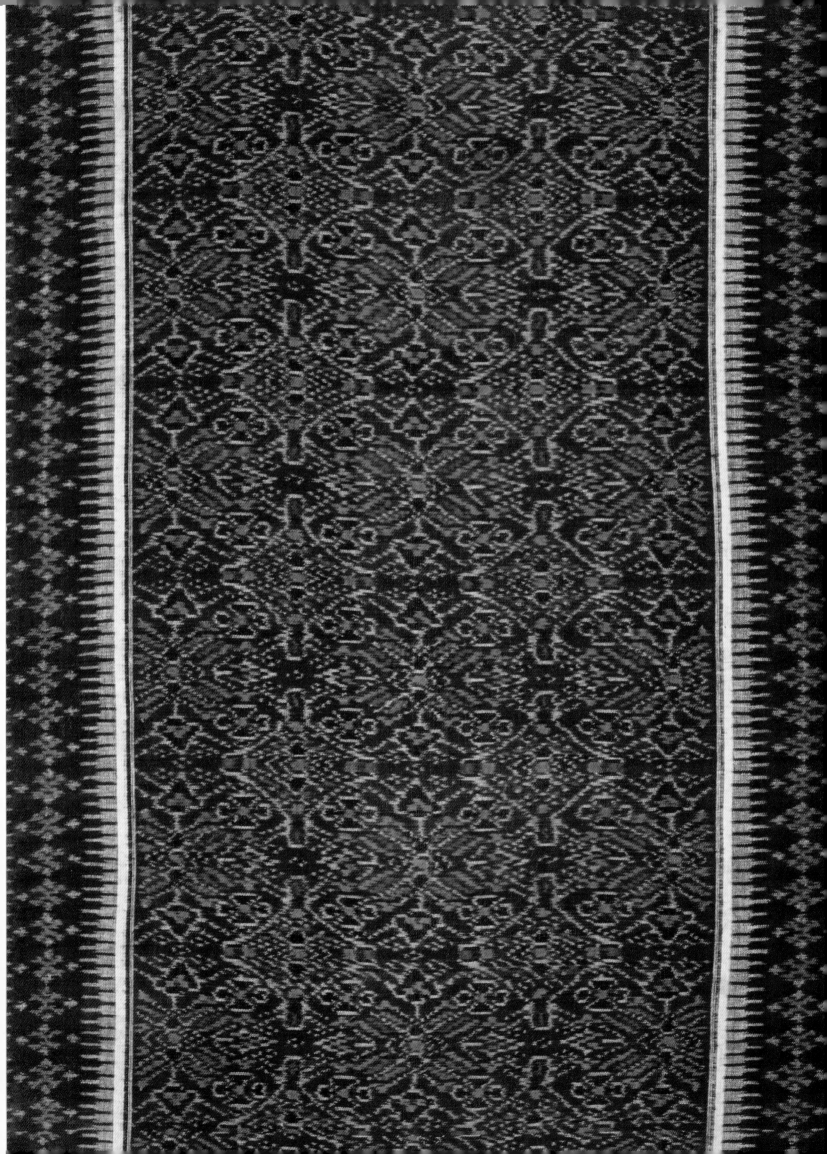

CHAPTER EIGHT

Cepuk

Sacred Textiles from Bali and Nusa Penida

PURIFICATORY, protective, defensive, strong, magical and dire— these are some of the ambiguous notions evoked whenever *cepuk* cloths are discussed in Bali, be it with priests, specialists in sacrificial offerings (*tukang banten*), traditional healers and soothsayers (*balian, dukun*), Rangda dancers, or simply with men and women of the older generation. It is rare to catch sight of these textiles at rituals and festivals now. Even if present, they get lost in a multi-hued profusion of *songkèt, perada, endek*, batik, *polèng* textiles and gaudy plastic wall hangings, all in the now-dominant gold, yellow-and-white and black-and-white coloring of ritual textiles.

What does the name *cepuk* mean, what do these mysterious cloths of yore look like, and what has become of them today? Literally, *cepuk* means "to meet, to encounter," or more clearly in its passive form *cepuk-ang*, "to be brought face to face with something," more precisely with divine powers. The word also signifies a class of ritual fabrics with four colors. In the latter case, it is usual to prefix another word indicating the precise function of the cloth, whether as an article of clothing for the living or the dead, as a ritual object, or as decoration for religious buildings and shrines. For example, *kamben* (wraparound cloth), *tapih* (inner hip cloth), *tatakan* (cloth on which to place offerings) or *iderider* (decorative band for the lintel of a building or shrine) may all be made of *cepuk* cloth. *Cepuk* may also be followed by a word characterizing features of the pattern or its particular ritual function. For instance, *cepuk arjuna* contains a figural representation of the hero Arjuna (see Fig. 8.4); and *cepuk cenana kawi* is a *cepuk* with a pattern said to represent *kawi* sandalwood (see Fig. 8.1 and Chapter 5).

The structural design principle is the same for all *cepuk* fabrics: a red background; a strictly patterned frame of fine white, black, blue and yellow lines; a center field and framing borders with geometric or abstract floral *ikat* patterns produced by the *endek* technique (see Chapter 2). There are variations, however, in the size of the cloths (ranging anywhere from 1.20 to 2.50 meters in length), as well as in the proportions between the center field and the framing borders, in the materials used (coarse handspun cotton or more refined industrial yarns, or more rarely silk), and in the shade of the background color (varying from deep purple or brownish-red to shades of earthy brick-red and vivid flame-red). No *cepuk* is complete, though, without the rows of white arrowheads

Figure 8.1 (opposite and above): *Kamben cepuk cenana kawi.* Presumably Tabanan, Kerambitan, late 19th century. 248 x 80 cm. MEB IIc 13940.

marking off longitudinal bands along the sides. Even today, these are still generally referred to as *gigi barong*, the teeth of the mighty, protective Barong spirit.

Until the late 1930s all the individual stripes and bands on the borders of *cepuk* still had names of associative significance, but knowledge of these has now faded into obscurity. Such conceptual systems reflected, on the one hand, the idea of the cloth as a human presence, with a head, eyebrows, lips and a smile. On the other hand, the whole configuration of the frame was seen as an architectural structure with the names of lines, contours and stepped plinths corresponding to the names of elements in the household shrines or guardian figures in the temple. Just as the former profusion of *ikat* patterns has been reduced to a few surviving types and a handful of new figural creations, so the knowledge of many *cepuk* pattern names and ritual functions has been lost to memory.

Within these strict structural principles, the variety of *ikat* patterns employed is quite astonishing, showing that the tradition of *cepuk* weaving has a long history and a wide regional distribution. Among the older cotton *cepuk* alone there are more than twenty different types of center field patterns, each with its variants. Lozenges, stars, crosses, geometrically stylized flowers and blossoming twigs cover the center field with a dense network of small repeats. Names such as "*saksak* blossom," "lotus flower," "*angket* grass" (Fig. 8.5), "*cemara* tree," "fragrant sandalwood" (Fig. 8.1), "dispersed starlets" or "love spell" usually evoke the association of these patterns with natural phenomena and plants, especially with those used in sacrificial rituals. A variety of motifs is also used in the lengthwise bands between the rows of *gigi barong*; for example, "*julit* blossom" (Fig.

Figure 8.2: Ni Nyoman Rentis using toothed bamboo sticks to dab on black. Nusa Penida.

8.1), "*bakung* leaves," "*kapu-kapu* tendril," and "frog's legs." The reader desirous of further information is referred to an earlier study of these motifs based on the collection in the Basel Museum of Ethnography (Nabholz 1989). The interpretation of certain parts of the pattern as anthropomorphic figures appears to be the invention of enterprising dealers; none of the many Balinese informants consulted recognized these as human figures.

In Nusa Penida, seven traditional patterns are still known and woven today. Weavers there often refer to the white rows of arrowheads as *pangoh taji*, "metal spurs of fighting cocks," instead of *gigi barong*. Around 1987 some weavers began to produce larger figural designs—elephants, for example—and mythical figures such as Arjuna (Fig. 8.4), Rama, or the rice goddess Déwi Sri. These new creations, however, seem to serve purely decorative rather than ritual purposes. They occasionally surface in art shops in Kuta or Sanur, where they are sometimes traded as antiques.

In Denpasar only a single workshop continues to produce *cepuk*, which are all of the same time; these have rather indistinct patterns, as can be seen in Figures 8.7 through 8.9. Lastly, one of the local palaces (*puri*) in Denpasar produces very cheap, small *cepuk* cloths of rayon, the *ikat* patterns of which are confined to a few white patches in the center field.

ARCHAIC AND ELABORATE PRODUCTION METHODS

Watching the complex and time-consuming work of making *cepuk* cloths is fascinating. It gives outsiders a better understanding of the reason why such power is thought to be latent in these fabrics. This applies in the first instance to the raw material used. Old *cepuk* cloths—and in Balinese eyes these are the most potent—are woven from locally grown cotton that is handspun and yields a rather coarse, yet resistant and vivid material. Until the 1960s, cotton was still grown on the dry Bukit peninsula in the south of Bali, in the *ladang* fields around Kerambitan in Tabanan, and especially on the island of Nusa Penida, where the dry and porous soils are particularly suited to its cultivation. Today, however, other agricultural products yield a higher income, and the amount of cotton grown is hardly enough to supply all the handspun yarns needed to produce fabrics for ritual purposes.

Even back in the 1930s, industrially spun cotton began to be imported from Java. At first it was used for the monochrome border stripes and then, with increasing frequency, for the patterned center fields. Imported silk was always the luxurious exception. Silken *cepuk* fabrics were made in north Bali (Bulèlèng) and also, more rarely, in the princely courts of Tabanan in west Bali. These remained the coveted prerogative of princely families. Since the 1950s, modern times have also overtaken the archaic *cepuk* cloths. It is increasingly common now for the bazaars of the capital to sell fabrics of staple yarn (*benang los*) or even of the cheapest rayon fibers; the more expensive products of cotton yarn (*benang gos*) are already beyond the means of most customers.

If we take as our starting point the complex manufacturing process used in a village in Gianyar in the 1930s (described in great detail by Bühler 1943), and add to it information on conditions before World War II given by older weavers from Kerambitan (Tabanan), comparing them with methods used today in a village in the remote highlands of Nusa Penida,

Figure 8.3: Ni Wayan Kerti weaving a *cepuk pancit genggong.* Nusa Penida.

Figure 8.4: Modern *cepuk* cloth with representation of Arjuna, woven in 1989 by Ni Nyoman Rentis. Nusa Penida. 106 x 85 cm. MEB IIc 20734.

we find that there have actually been few basic changes. As an example, I shall describe below the work of Ni Nyoman Rentis, a deft and gifted weaving woman in Nusa Penida, to show how she goes about her demanding task. This is not a full-time job for her; she also has chores in the house compound and in the plant garden; moreover, her services as an expert on sacrifical offerings are in great demand.

To produce eight double *kamben cepuk*, each about two meters in length, Ni Nyoman Rentis has to spend almost two weeks on preparatory work before she can start any weaving at all. For one whole day she winds the weft yarns on a rotatable tying frame (*penamplikan*) which is the width of the cloths to be woven, and arranges and fixes the continuous threads in sets in accordance with the pattern. All the sets together produce a patterned repeat recurring 11 to 19 times in the finished cloth. Then, for five more days, she binds the sets with plastic strips in all those places which are not to be dyed red or dabbed with black and yellow. Previously, strips of young banana bast (*kupas*) were used for this purpose.

The dyeing process now follows in several stages, taking three days to complete. For the red base color, the weft sets are wholly immersed in a dye bath, hung up and then dried. After the sets have been carefully arranged and all the tyings for black and yellow parts removed, these two colors are applied to the opened areas with the aid of small toothed bamboo sticks (*penyatrian*) and then rubbed into the yarn bundles (see Fig. 8.2). Today only cheap synthetic dyes are used—naphthol for the red bath, and cheap direct dyestuffs obtainable from the bazaars of Klungkung and Denpasar for dabbing on. These synthetic dyestuffs gained acceptance in Bali at an extraordinarily early date; in 1908 a Dutch author reported ugly and garish aniline dyes on *endek* fabrics at Bulèlèng in north Bali. However, it was not until the 1930s that they were first seen on the archaic *cepuk* cloths of Nusa Penida. Beginning with the monochrome border stripes, they had, by the 1950s, completely displaced vegetable dyes even there. Synthetic dyes are a success not so much because of their vibrant colors and wider range of shades, but rather because they are infinitely simpler and quicker to use.

Traditional vegetable dyes demanded careful pretreatment of the yarns with mordants and oils, which impart a soft, yellowish tint of their own. Red dye was obtained by mixing the pounded outside layers of the roots of *Morinda citrifolia* (called *sunti* or *tibah*) with the rind *Baccaurea racemosa*, oil from candlenuts (*Aleurites mollucana*) and other ingredients in water, and then straining out the residues. The bundle of yarn had to be steeped at least ten times in a freshly prepared mixture, kneaded and then dried, until a rich deep red was obtained. For blue shades, use was made of indigo leaves (*taum*) mixed with lime, ginger and various leaves, while a mixture of turmeric (*kunyit*), lemon juice and pineapple leaves was used for yellow. Violet and green were obtained by double dyeing, and soot from burned coconut shells and candlenuts was added to the indigo bath to obtain black. These colors could not be applied directly but only by immersing the yarns in vats, and apart from the time spent preparing the dye baths, several time-consuming applications were thus usually necessary.

When the patterning is completed, the yarns are hung up to be dried, brushed, arranged and separately spooled on weft bobbins according to the repeats in the design. The plain red warp with its border stripes in different colors is then warped on the conventional Balinese warping device (*penganyinan*) consisting of a long beam with vertical pegs (Figs. 3.9 and 3.10). For about a day Ni Nyoman Rentis winds the warp threads to and fro on the pegs, while at the same time crossing the threads and forming sheds for the simple weaving method using shed stick and heddle rod. Here again a labor-saving innovation has been introduced: whereas previously it was the custom to work at a warping device only about two meters wide with a to-and-fro rocking motion, a much longer apparatus is now used and the weaver walks from one end to the other.

Weaving is still done on the traditional *cagcag* loom (Figs. 3.11 and 8.3) that is also in general use for *songkèt* home weaving (see Chapter 3) and sometimes for producing *endek*. In Nusa Penida it is still frequently fitted with an artistically carved yoke and hung with bells that tinkle in rhythm with the weaving. Setting up the warp and entering each individual thread in the reed takes Ni Nyoman Rentis another two days. Then at last everything is ready: she needs two more days working from early morning until nightfall to weave a double *kamben cepuk*. It used to take three days with cotton yarn. For the pattern to be clearly defined and attractive, each weft pick must be carefully placed. The vertical white strips that are invariably placed along the edges are a useful guide.

Developments of the last sixty years have been aimed at saving labor and

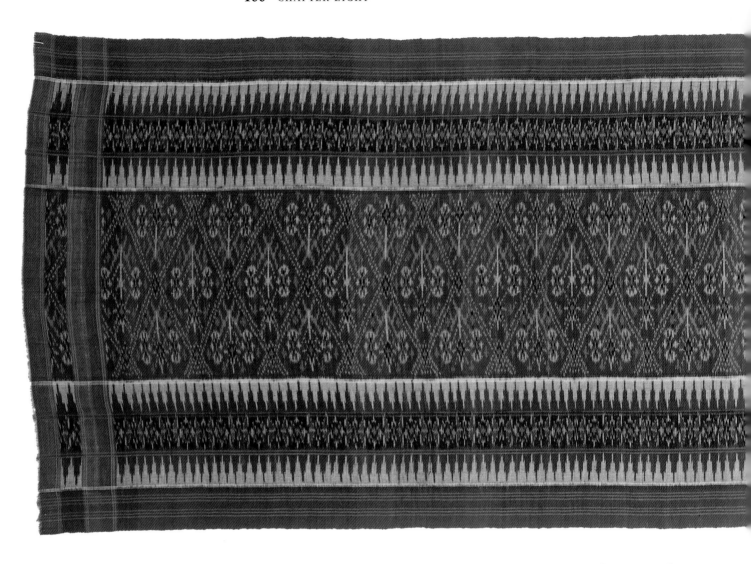

Figure 8.5: *Kamben cepuk padang angket.*
South Bali, c. 1900. 240 x 76 cm.
MEB IIc 14948.

cost in all steps along the way. Cheaper and more resistant factory-made yarns, synthetic tying materials, quick-acting synthetic dyestuffs and longer warps are all in demand. Logically enough, *cepuk* cloths are also now being made on modern ATBM looms (see Chapter 2) with high-speed weft bobbins in the capital city of Denpasar.

Needless to say, all of this has been achieved at a cost—in quality, aesthetics and variety of patterns used. A comparison of fine old *cepuk* cloths (Figs. 8.1, 8.5, 8.12) with modern ones (Fig. 8.4) shows the differences only too clearly, and one may readily appreciate why many Balinese deny that the new cloths possess the inherent power of the older ones. In my mind's eye I can still see a young man from a princely family in north Tabanan taking a gaudy modern *cepuk* in his hands, letting the material gently slip a few times through his fingers, sniffing at it, and then shaking his head vigorously in dismay: "No that's not a proper *cepuk*, that's not a cloth you can use for rituals." And I still have ringing in my ears the laughter of weavers in Nusa Penida, who on seeing a cloth bought in Denpasar exclaimed: "Oh no! That's not a proper *cepuk*. That's been made by a child or a beginner!" Yet here again we find the Balinese broad-minded and adaptable, as in the remark made by one of the wives of the late raja of Tabanan, who died in 1987: "If we no longer have an old *cepuk*, we can make do with a new one. Only fanatics object to the use of such modern cloths in rituals."

So it makes good sense to handle old *cepuk* cloths with extreme care.

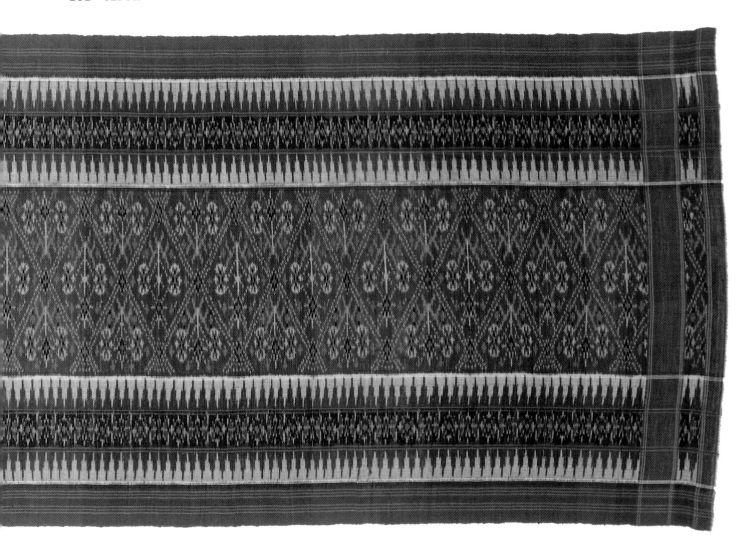

They are kept as precious family heirlooms like other ritual objects such as *lontar* texts and family krisses. When tattered and torn, they are not simply discarded, like objects without a soul. In Kerambitan, the officiating priest of the Pura Dalem in 1939 took the temple *cepuk*, which had been ravaged by insects, and burned it to ashes so that it would pass on to the next world. Quite a few families keep shreds of tattered *cepuk* cloths for years up in the roof beams of their rice granaries. People rarely and only reluctantly lend sacred cloths for rituals outside of their own house compounds, for fear they might disappear and find their way into the hands of an astute and unscrupulous dealer, to be sold off in an antique shop at a phenomenal price to some Western or Japanese collector.

RAIMENTS FOR HUMANS AND ANCESTORS

Personal observations at numerous rituals and festivities, conversations with village chiefs responsible for the application of customary law (*kelian adat*), and discussions with soothsaying healers (*balian*) and women versed in the art of sacrificial offerings (*tukang banten*), have yielded a clear picture of the role played by *cepuk* cloths as festive raiment in ritual ceremonies (*panca yadnya*), in dramatic performances, in traditional healing, and in the royal investiture ceremonies. Or to be more correct: played *in the past*, for time and time again one hears the phrase: ". . . if anyone still owns a *cepuk*!" A few examples will help to flesh out the current situation, and some additional comments will throw light on the principles of *cepuk* use within the ritual system.

Figure 8.6: Cremation tower with a *cepuk* cloth as an underlay for the corpse of a priest of Pura Luhur Batukaru. Tabanan, Wongayagedé.

So far, little mention of *cepuk* cloths has been found in the written Balinese sources. A traditional text, the *Babad Blahbatu*, relates that the *ksatria* hero I Gusti Ngurah Jelantik, acting on the orders of the ruler of Gèlgèl, took the field against the East Javanese forces of Blangbangan in a protective combat dress consisting of a white head cloth of silk, a *songkèt* with a red background around his loins, and a *cepuk sari*—presumably worn over a wraparound cloth. The word *sari*, meaning "flowers, essence of offerings," was still used in the 1930s to designate a *cepuk* with rows of lozenges in the center field. It was also I Gusti Ngurah Jelantik who, on behalf of the same *dalem* of Gèlgèl, subdued the last ruler of Nusa Penida (I Dalem Bungkut), through the use of magic weapons, thus bringing the island under the hegemony of Gèlgèl. Similarly, in a version of the East Javanese *Malat* epic of the 14th and 15th centuries it is related that the hero, Prince Panji, wore a *cepuk* as a *sabuk* or sash.

In former times it was quite common for men and women to wear *cepuk* as part of their ceremonial attire when they had occasion to enter the princely *puri* and *jero* of Klungkung or Tabanan. It is rare nowadays for people to wear *cepuk* fabrics at festivals in this manner, but it does happen—especially in Nusa Penida. There a man may be seen at a temple anniversary festival in Batunungul, or at a mass cremation in Semaya, wearing the archaic cloth as a *saput* wound around his hip cloth. Or a woman may appear at a grand annual festival (*usaba*) after the harvest in the temple of Dalem Peed with a carefully folded *cepuk* girded as a *seléndang* over her blouse. Among the more than 700 women celebrating a great festival for the purification of the souls of long-dead ancestors (*mukur*) in Sanur, circling in procession (*pradaksina*) three times around the central Brahmanic compound bearing wonderfully ornamented effigies on their heads (*puspalingga*), there was only one who had chosen a *cepuk* as an undergarment (see Fig. 8.7). All the others wore white or white and yellow clothing, although with an additional underskirt of precious *perada* material (Fig. 1.6). On the other hand it is still relatively common to see *cepuk* cloths on the Galungan and Kuningan holy days when, as underlays, they are also used to provide a ritually clean place for the rich sacrificial offerings.

At the small princely court of Biaung in the north of the district of Tabanan, *cepuk* cloths are used in the important *nigang sasihin* ritual (see Chapter 5 for a description of this ceremony). When the little daughter of one of the sons of the noble family was three Balinese months old (105 days) a large company of guests attended the feast. The closest relatives gathered in the family shrine shortly after midday. A Brahman priest then performed the complicated offerings and rituals for the

Figure 8.7 (left): Young woman from Denpasar in *adat* attire wearing a *cepuk* wrapped under her skirt at a soul-purifying ceremony (*mukur*) for hundreds of deceased ancestors. Sanur.

Figure 8.8 (right): Dead woman of the *wésia* caste, laid out under plaited bamboo, white cloth and a *cepuk* cloth. South Tabanan.

purification and physical and spiritual strengthening of the child. Next to the raised *balé*, where the priest performed his rites, was a small table with the important offerings, ritual artifacts and bowls of holy water placed on a *cepuk* which, as an underlay (*tatakan*), purified the area.

Cepuk cloths suspended from the ceiling performed a similar function at a six-month festival for a child from Batununggul in Nusa Penida. Along with checked *keling* fabrics, batik materials and *ikat* fabrics from Sumba, they adorned and also protected all the many and varied offerings and ritual objects standing in a pile. It was also formerly the practice among distinguished families in the Tabanan area to bury the afterbirth (*ari-ari*) in the house compound shortly after birth, wrapped in a *cepuk*. A *cepuk* was also wrapped around the rice mortar (*lesung*) supporting a clay vessel containing the child's purifying bath of holy water during the first "birthday" ceremony. In Denpasar, Bangli and Kusamba (in Klungkung)

Figure 8.9: Principal shrine of the goddess Ratu Kahyangan Sakti (Durga) at a temple festival after renovation (*melaspas*). Sanur.

the child itself was enveloped in a *cepuk* as a protective wraparound. This was done, however, only if the ancestor reincarnated in the child had made known his wishes explicitly through a *balian* trance medium, or if the child had lost an older or younger brother or sister by death and was thus in particular jeopardy (*sanan empeg*). In Nusa Penida a child was protected during such rituals by covering it with a *cepuk* as a blanket. In a six-month ritual performed at the remote mountain village of Tulad, such a cloth—along with hand-spun yarn, *képéng* coins, a small coconut, unboiled rice, cloves and an egg—were placed inside a plaited basket. This *daksina* was set up on the roof of the kitchen where the child was born. At the beginning of the ritual, the priest summoned the soul of the child to leave the sea via the sun, Surya, and to enter this *daksina*.

In tooth-filing ceremonies (*matatah*), *cepuk* again primarily serve a protective function. This is a rite of passage of primary importance in which young men and women, usually during puberty, have the lower edges of their upper teeth filed off with small chisels and grindstones so they are more even. The purpose is to suppress the influence of the *sad ripu*, the six inner enemies of mankind (see Chapter 5). Spread out as an underlay (*tatakan*) during the ceremony, *cepuk* cloths keep polluting and baleful influences away from offerings or ritual meals with six different flavors (*padamel*).

At the same time they afford protection to persons undergoing tooth filing: as an awning over the place of filing, as a decoration around the pillars, as an underlay for the recumbent person (Fig. 3.6), as a covering over the pillow supporting the head or—instead of the more common checked *selulut* fabrics (see Chapter 5)—as a *tatindih* covering the entire body of the celebrant up to the chin. It is exceptional for *cepuk* to be worn as part of the *adat* attire in this ritual, as underskirts or sashes for women, or as an outer hip cloth for men. It may be that they are needed only by people who are at particular risk, e.g. the *sanan empeg*, as described above.

At tooth-filing ceremonies and weddings conducted in the princely courts of Kerambitan and Tabanan the main celebrants may on no account be in contact with the ground during the ritual. It was therefore previously the custom to lay down *cepuk* cloths to make a path leading from the place of ritual to the family shrine free from all possible baleful influences. Thus the late raja of Tabanan, who died in 1987, stepped only on *cepuk* cloths during his ceremonial investiture (*mabiseka ratu*) in 1945. The custom of laying down an undefiled path with white, or more rarely also with *polèng* cloths (see Chapter 7, Fig. 7.14), is still observed today in temples during the procession of the gods. The use of *cepuk* cloths, on the other hand, was always confined to the courts.

By and large, however, it is becoming increasingly rare to use *cepuk* at tooth filings and weddings. Its purificatory and protective function is now performed by white-and-yellow cloths but, even more important—or so the older generation says—is the fact that the archaic and rather

Figure 8.10: Large *caru* offering for demons with *kerbau* (water buffalo) under white and black material and *cepuk* cloth at a purification ceremony for the souls of ancestors. Denpasar.

coarse *cepuk* fabrics are no longer felt to be up-to-date and aesthetically pleasing to the younger generation. Its place is increasingly being taken by more delicate, colored batik and *endek* cloths, or by glittering *songkèt* fabrics and their cheaper imitations.

Nevertheless, *cepuk* are still used in death rituals, as illustrated by the following two examples:

Three days after the death of the wife of the headman of a large *wésia* clan in a village in southern Tabanan, her relatives performed the first in a long and elaborate series of rituals to release and purify the soul (*pitra yadnya*). These occur over a number of years, culminating in the long-awaited moment when the soul takes up abode in the family shrine in a pure, deified state and is reborn in a child. In the first stage, the body, which is regarded merely as a temporary vessel for the spirit (*atma*), is purified. The next day it is consigned to the flames and returned to the five elements whence it came. The soul is thus freed from its mortal, material frame. Some sixty family members assemble in the narrow compound. There is much busy to-ing and fro-ing in a light-hearted, cheerful and colorful atmosphere, free of visible signs of mourning, tears or apprehension. This does not mean, however, that the relatives feel no grief at the death; it is simply that sorrow must not be displayed in public, for mourning would be an impediment to the soul's passage to the next world (*swarga*).

Under the direction of a priest the relatives wash the corpse with holy water, and then decorate and bedizen it with flowers, tiny mirrors and small offerings. Then they enshroud it in many layers of white cloth and batik fabrics, followed by a palm-leaf mat covering and a rigid wicker-work of bamboo. The bundle is laid out amidst offerings and ritual objects, and over it are spread more white cloths with, on the top, a *cepuk* as *tatindih* (low Balinese *rurub*) (Fig. 8.8). This was formerly burned with the corpse. Today it is saved for further use but, after the cremation, it must be ritually purified with holy water, offerings and a special mantra uttered by a priest. With the aid of this *mantra perascita*, all the gods are invoked in meditation to purify and lustrate the remains of deceased ancestors.

Another *cepuk* cloth played an important role in a funeral ritual in Wongayagedé, a village in north Tabanan. The eldest and most renowned priest of the famous mountain temple Pura Luhur Batukaru had died a few days before. His corpse was carried to the graveyard on a high tower (*wadah*) resting on a *cepuk* to keep off malevolent forces (Fig. 8.6).

In other villages of Tabanan, Badung and Klungkung, depending on the status of the family, whole *cepuk* cloths or small fragments are placed under the corpse or laid around the body or only on the face or the genitals. Less wealthy families use cheaper rayon cloths from Denpasar with a rudimentary *cepuk* pattern. In the Puri Agung of Tabanan it was formerly the custom to wrap the deceased's ashes in *cepuk* and cast them into the sea.

The potency of *cepuk* cloths can also be employed for curative and magic purposes. As recorded in *lontar* texts, such practices form a portion of the occult knowledge of traditional healers and soothsayers (*balian, dukun*). For instance, ashes from a few burned *cepuk* threads (they may in fact

simply be ordinary silk threads) are mixed with coconut oil or milk from a young coconut and with leaves from the *timul* tree, then rubbed into the skin or given as a drench to cure cows that are off their feed or have diarrhea. Patients with respiratory spasms are thought to benefit from drinking or being rubbed with water containing the leaves of medicinal plants into which a *cepuk* thread has been inserted. Magic potions made of water and ashes from a burned piece of *cepuk* can help the lovesick to attain the object of their desire. However, all these practices are thought to be effective only in conjunction with special mantras and offerings, and only old *cepuk* cloths, already used in ceremonies (*wali*), can be employed for this purpose; modern *cepuk* are devoid of such curative and supernatural powers.

CEPUK FOR GODS AND DEMONS

Just as humans have many divine traits, so the gods and demons are in many ways like humans, and in rituals their human aspects must receive consideration. Thus they are fed, bathed, perfumed with fragrant essences, dressed and adorned—very often with *cepuk* cloths.

In a village in southern Tabanan the village temple and both *balé barong* and *angklung* celebrate the anniversary festival (*odalan*). The masks of both Jero Gedé (Barong) and Jero Luh (Rangda) and other masks for the Calon Arang drama are set up on a large platform amidst a profusion of offerings. In the very center stands the *pralingga* of the village temple, a seat for the gods and ancestors who have achieved divine status. The construction is artistically garlanded with flowers, hand-spun yarn, *képéng* coins and a face of silver, and is draped with white cloths, *perada*

Figure 8.11: *Cepuk* cloth of silk. Bulèlèng, c. 1900. 120 x 79 cm. MEB IIc 20299.

Figure 8.12 (following pages): *Kamben cepuk tangkariga* or *kartika*. Presumably Tabanan, Kerambitan, 1920-30. 125 x 74 cm. (not complete) MEB IIc 13939.

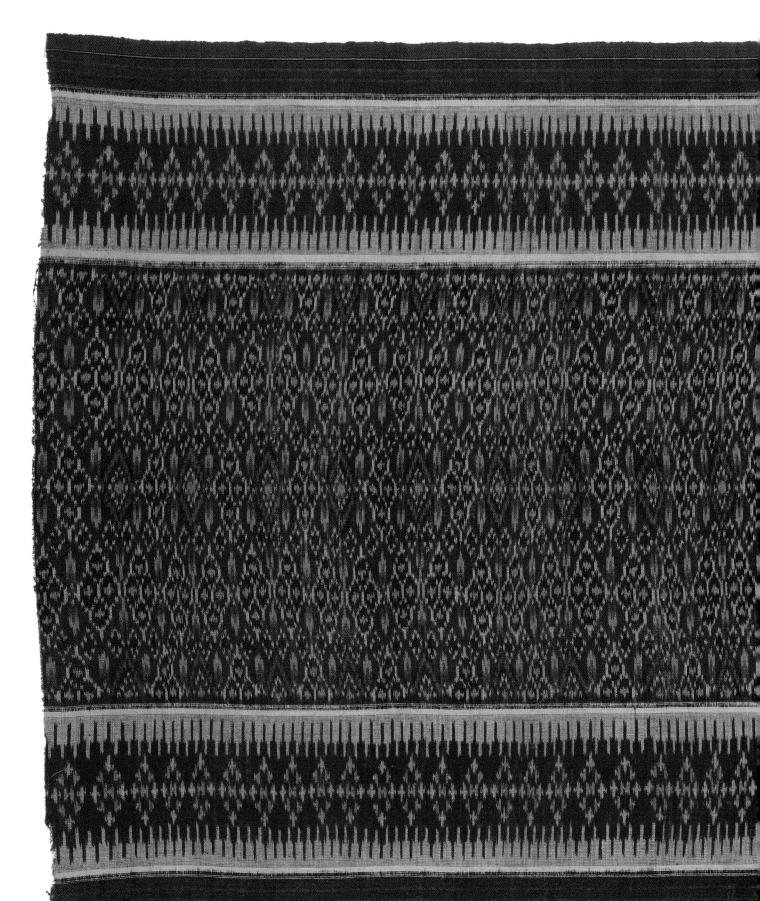

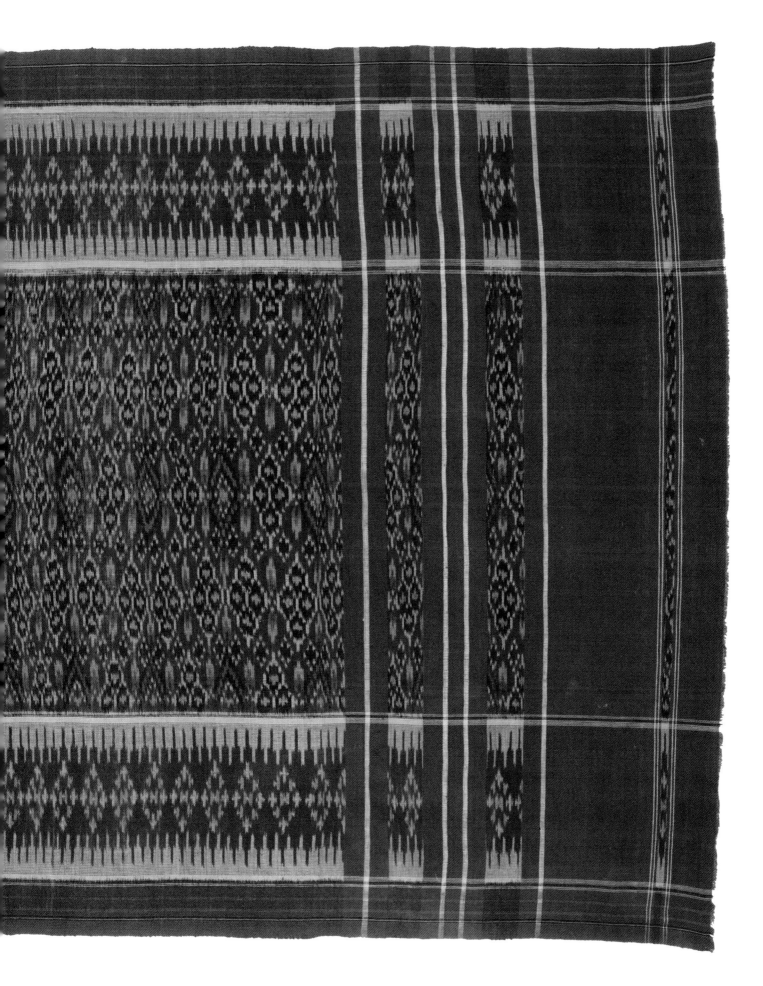

fabrics and a *cepuk* wound around it as a *sinjang* undergarment (low Balinese *tapih*). Similarly, at festivals in a graveyard temple in Sanur, the likeness of the goddess Ratu Kahyangan Sakti (Durga) is decorated with two *cepuk* cloths wrapped and draped one over the other (Fig. 8.9).

A few days later one of the village priests of Kerambitan consecrates the family shrine in his own compound. He has had existing shrines renovated and new ones added, and now has to purify the place defiled by these operations by means of a *melaspas* ritual in which the gods and ancestors are asked to descend. On a centrally located platform stand innumerable offerings and richly decorated *sekah*, which are baskets conceived to be symbolic abodes for ancestors raised to divine status. To ensure the ritual purity of the place, the offerings are laid on a *cepuk*, an old checked cloth with a black ground and a red center field (*kamben sara*), as well as on white-and-yellow fabrics spread one over the other.

In another village in Tabanan, it was once the custom to drape white cloth and hand-spun strands of cotton around the male, and a *cepuk* around the female *taman bebangkit*. This couple, constructed of sugarcane stalks and colored rice cakes, is a symbolic representation of the cosmos—the world and the planets—and is displayed at temple festivals dedicated to the goddess Durga and the underworld *kala* demons.

The use to which a *cepuk* is put at a temple festival on the Bukit peninsula of Bali is particularly impressive. After illness had struck several members of his family and his business was in a bad way, a rich hotel proprietor of Denpasar recalled an oath on which his father had reneged, and so, at the anniversary festival of the famous Pura Luhur Uluwatu temple, he donated a *caru agung* offering so as to mollify and propitiate the demons of the underworld. This was an oblation of the very highest level and, besides countless sacrificial offerings, it included a *kerbau* (water buffalo) covered by a *cepuk* cloth.

In a similar way, all the women carrying the symbols of their ancestors on the occasion of an important purification ceremony (*mukur*) in Denpasar had to walk over a *caru agung* offering containing a *kerbau* (water buffalo) covered with an old *cepuk* cloth (Fig. 8.10).

Figure 8.13 (above): Performer personifying Rangda with *cepuk* as wraparound skirt, shortly before the beginning of a Calon Arang drama. South Tabanan.

Figure 8.14 (above right): Temporary shrine with Barong Kèt and Rangda masks, hung with *cepuk* cloths, at a *melis* ritual by the sea. South Bali, north of Legian.

Just as black-and-white checked *polèng* cloths are associated with the giant Barong Landung masked figures of the netherworld (see Chapter 7), *cepuk* cloths are invariably connected with the mighty and fearsome figure of Rangda. As in villages all along the southern coast of Bali, an annual event is celebrated in a village north of Legian just before Nyepi, the first day of the *saka* year, when all the gods are borne from the village temples to the sea in a great *melis* procession. The purpose is to purify each village and to guard it against the dire influences of Ratu Gedé Mas Mecaling and his demon hordes from Nusa Penida. Represented with the others are the giant Barong Landung and also the masks of Barong Kèt, the Rangdas and other demons of the netherworld whose strength is to be replenished and made use of. Small temporary shrines, splendidly decorated with golden cloths and bobbing sprays of leaves, are borne on carrying frames by dozens of men (see Fig. 8.14). Here can be seen a Barong Kèt with its head veiled; inside the shrines and out of

Figure 8.15: Rangda instructs a pupil in witchcraft (*sisia*). Gianyar, Saba.

sight are the Rangda masks and masks of other netherworld gods concealed behind a fluttering curtain of *cepuk* which affords protection from their demonic forces.

The exorcistic powers of *cepuk* cloths are most clearly apparent in Rangda's attire. She is revered as a protectress and helper, and deferentially addressed by the titles Jero Luh (in Tabanan) or Batari Durga (in Nusa Penida). She also inspires fear, figuring in dramatic performances of purification and restoration of the divine order, when witchcraft, disease, unnatural death or drought have prevailed or crops have failed. She embodies the primordial image of the widow, and is the queen of all witches; she represents the negative black magic of the left and is also held to be the incarnation of the goddess Durga. Under the terrifying mask, with its wildly flying mane, she conceals magical clothing which invests her with demonic powers and, at the same time, protects her from the Barong Jero Gedé and the naked weapons of his aggressive escort. Over trousers and a shirt, trimmed with strips of red and black cloth and animal fur, the accompanying priest winds a physically and magically efficacious breastplate consisting of yards of white, black and black-and-white checked strips, between which her breasts protrude and dangle (Fig. 8.13). And as with the representation of the goddess Durga in Sanur (Fig. 8.9), a *cepuk* is wound around her hips as an undergarment (*sinjang*, low Balinese *tapih*) that serves to highlight the seminudity of her repulsive body. This *cepuk* is replete with active magical power. No dancer, however strong, would ever dare to incarnate the endangered but terrifying figure of Rangda without this protection. Before a cloth can perform this exorcistic function it must, like the mask itself, be infused with power (*pasupati*) by a priest, who uses special mantras and offerings in a cemetery or mortuary temple at midnight on certain days. Its potency is further enhanced by the use of handspun Balinese yarn (*benang Bali*) and archaic vegetable dyestuffs in four sacred colors. Only then, according to what priests and Rangda dancers tell us, does it acquire the odium of "significant and outstanding, precious and sacred, and at the same time uncanny and hideous (*serem*)."

Certain exceptions to these established rules are already observable. Old *cepuk* can be replaced by new ones if the latter have been properly charged with power in a ritual. One Rangda figure in Kerambitan, and some of the many Rangda figures from the Denpasar area and Sanur which are replenished with new vigor every year at the Pengerebongan festival in Kesiman, now wear *ikat* cloths from eastern Sumba instead of *cepuk*. Being mysterious products of an alien island culture to the east, they can apparently assume this function. There is one other interesting exception. In the very mountain village in Nusa Penida where *cepuk* is still woven, two Rangda figures—Batari Durga and Batari Istri—appear on Kuningan in yellow or dark-green and gold-striped wraparound cloths rather than *cepuk*. Even in earlier times, it is said they never wore *cepuk*. It is as if the locally made fabrics lacked the necessary power.

MYSTERIOUS POWER OF THE CLOTHS

The significance and power of *cepuk* cloths is thus to be seen in their use in rituals as barriers keeping dangerous forces at bay, embuing a place with purity, protecting human beings in dangerous situations, purifying them, making them strong and invulnerable, and playing an active role as magical and curative objects. These powers they derive from the raw

Figure 8.16 (opposite): *Kamben cepuk padma*, upper part without clear pattern (*nori reges* or *ucik*). Presumably Tabanan, Kerambitan, early 20th century. 143 x 78 cm. (not complete) MEB IIc 13941.

materials used—handspun yarn of ancient Balinese origin—as well as the elaborate dyeing process employing old vegetable dyestuffs. But there are other important sources of their power as well: the similarity they bear to powerful *patola* cloths—double *ikat* silk fabrics of Indian origin—and the symbolism of their coloring, as well as their associations with certain divinities.

Over many centuries *patola* cloths imported from India have figured importantly in many areas of the Indonesian archipelago as precious family heirlooms and cult artifacts of the highest value. They were copied in many local weaving traditions—and in Bali this has resulted in *cepuk* cloths. The similarities in structure, coloring and even individual patterns are unmistakable. This is particularly evident in the example of *cepuk cenana kawi* (Fig. 8.1), which derives from a classical *patola* motif. Many examples are known in which *cepuk* cloths replace the rare *patola* in rituals.

The supernatural powers of *cepuk* fabrics also derive from their colors. The cloths are always given the four cardinal colors of white, red, yellow and blue (alternatively black or green) and, as an overall effect, the entire color spectrum combined. These colors are correlated with the divinities Iswara in the east, Brahma in the south, Mahadewa in the west, Wisnu in the north and Siwa in the center.

Finally, in the ideology of many Balinese, the mysterious *cepuk* cloths are associated with Nusa Penida, the origin of all evil and magic, personified in the divine and demonic figure of Ratu Gedé Mas Mecaling who, in the company of his myrmidons, annually visits the whole of Bali with crop failures, sickness and death. In actual fact Nusa Penida appears to have been a secondary place of *cepuk* production. It would seem rather that the art was diffused mainly from Klungkung, or the earlier kingdom of Gèlgèl, which subdued Nusa Penida and turned it into a place of banishment, only later perhaps reaching the principality of Bulèlèng. Many of the weavers in Nusa Penida belong to powerful *wésia* clan associations with connections in Klungkung, and also Tabanan and Badung. The two latter princely dynasties were related and also had close links with Klungkung. It is known that artisans from Tabanan served at the court of Klungkung, and that famous families of craftsmen in Tabanan trace their origins back to the princely line of the *ksatria dalem* ruling houses in Gèlgèl and Klungkung. And there can be no doubt that it was chiefly the princely courts which provided the home for the traditional manufacture and use of *cepuk* cloths, and to some extent this is still true today.

—*M.L. Nabholz-Kartaschoff*

CHAPTER NINE

Geringsing

Magical Protection and Communal Identity

IN the ancient, ritualistic (Bali Aga) society of Tenganan Pegeringsingan, the god Indra is honored as the creator of the first human beings and, at the same time, as the divine designer of a category of magical fabrics which are among the most spectacular ever produced by the textile art of Southeast Asia. The *geringsing* cloths of Tenganan, as they are called, have made this east Balinese village famous the world over among textile technologists. They are produced by what is known as the double *ikat* method—a technique in which resist patterns are applied to both the warp and weft before weaving, so that the final pattern appears only on completion. This demanding and time-consuming process is known in only three places in the world: India, Japan and Indonesia, while in the entire Indonesian archipelago it is practiced only in the tiny village of Tenganan Pegeringsingan.

"One evening, seated on a medicinal *selegui* shrub (*Sida rhombifolia*), Bhatara Indra was reveling in the radiance of the moonlight and the beauty of the stars. These resolved themselves into images and patterns which, from that time onward, were destined to become the sacred raiments of the first Balinese. The god Indra then taught the girls and women the art of making double *ikat* cloths." Since that time the magical *kamben geringsing* have become an indispensable part of the divine scheme which Indra ordained for Tenganan Pegeringsingan, as well as one of the most important ceremonial fabrics in Bali.

The god Indra selected the people of Tenganan to administer a territory that was conceived, in accordance with his divine plan, as an *imago mundi*—a microcosm of the world. They were instructed to use every available means to keep it pure and clean, and the concept of territorial, bodily and spiritual purity and integrity is of paramount importance in the culture of this village—reflected not only in a ritual intercourse with the surrounding territories (purifications, exorcisms), but also in the notion that only if a person is healthy in body and spirit may he or she participate in rituals. This is why no one with a disability may be admitted to the village *adat* organizations. Ritual apparel thus attests to the wearer's divine entitlement to membership in the Tenganan community, and evinces one's purity and eligibility to take part in communal rituals. Such purity is in turn effectively shielded from harmful or impure influences from outside by the magical, protective power of the cloths.

Figure 9.1: (opposite and above): *Geringsing lubèng* (one half of the cloth). Tenganan Pegeringsingan, presumably early 20th century. 168 x 119 cm., made by joining two widths of weaving. MEB IIc 18003.

Figure 9.2: Making a *geringsing sanan empeg* with the traditional horizontal back-strap loom. Tenganan Pegeringsingan.

Early this century, while visiting the palace of the prince of Tabanan, the Dutch explorer W. O. J. Nieuwenkamp became the first Westerner to encounter these "very remarkable fabrics" decorated with austere patterns in muted "ancient colors." They appeared to him to consist "not only of ikated weft threads but also, and this was the most curious feature of the discovery, of similarly processed warp threads." Learning in Karangasem—now Amlapura—that the cloths were made exclusively in the remote village of Tenganan Pegeringsingan, he hastened with a princely escort to investigate the matter, traveling first 17 kilometers westward along the coast, and then inland along hill paths in the direction of the divine volcano, Gunung Agung. After hours of hard riding he finally passed through a narrow gate into the village, its rows of house compounds tucked into a U-shaped valley and enclosed by walls and hedges. It is to this expedition on horseback, and the hospitality of the local people, that we are indebted for the first, albeit in many respects quite incomplete, information on the equipment, production techniques, colors and motifs of the *kamben geringsing*.

Since that time, the once narrow gates that admitted only one visitor at a time have been opened wide. A steadily growing stream of tourists now inundates the island of Bali, and has left its mark also on the conservative and ritualistic society of Tenganan Pegeringsingan—especially since the publication of a calendar of festivals, now easily attended from the new tourist resort of Candi Dasa nearby. In spite of these marked extraneous influences, however, the people of Tenganan have nevertheless succeeded thus far in keeping their ritual life virtually intact. And this includes, as already mentioned, the use of *kamben geringsing* as the showpieces of an elaborate ritual wardrobe.

FORMS AND FASHIONS

The most striking and characteristic feature of all *kamben geringsing* is their muted coloring—combining red and reddish-brown tones, eggshell and dark blue or black-violet. These are obtained by dyeing or cross-dyeing with pigments obtained from outer layers of the *sunti* root (*Morinda citrifolia*), and with *taum*, i.e. indigo. A certain uniformity in appearance is also due to the fact that the cloths are, without exception, woven in loose tabby from cotton yarns. Their "rustic" texture as compared with silk fabrics of Balinese provenance is further emphasized by the way designs are built up out of tiny rectangles (due to the way the patterning is produced by both thread systems together), and by the fact that the structure and architecture of the motifs extends over the entire surface of the cloths, producing patterns of great pictorial charm (Figs. 9.1, 9.13).

In addition to this general impression of structure, form and color, closer examination shows that there is a uniform principle of design that calls for dividing the surface area into two corresponding "head" portions at either end, leaving a large central panel that is in turn subdivided by arranging the motifs in various ways. For instance, horizontally and vertically oriented groups of geometric and abstract floral motifs may be repeated over the whole of the central field (*geringsing peparé, geringsing enjékan siap, geringsing batun tuung*) (Fig. 9.13). In other fabrics notable for their regularly repeating patterns composed of stylized flowers, lozenges, stars and small crosses, the principle of repetition is not confined to the horizontal and vertical directions but may also be pursued along the diagonals (*geringsing cicempaka, geringsing cemplong*) (Figs. 9.3, 9.4). The latter device may also be seen in narrow-strip cloths in which the motifs or groups of motifs are arranged in clearly distinguishable checked rectangles (*geringsing sidan pegat, geringsing sanan empeg*) (Fig. 9.2).

Central field patterns are formed in quite a different way in a category of cloths whose principal representative—the *wayang* type—has won renown in the world's museums (Fig. 9.15). Large four-pointed stars with a crenellated motif surrounded by four scorpions divide the main field into semicircular segments. These segments contain stars, emblems, architectural elements, animals and—in the style of East Javanese temple reliefs and Balinese *wayang kulit* figures—anthropomorphic figures in groups of twos and threes (*geringsing wayang kebo, geringsing wayang puteri, geringsing patelikur isi, geringsing lubèng*).

Figure 9.3: *Geringsing cicempaka petang dasa*. Tenganan Pegeringsingan, presumably late 19th century. 162 x 61 cm. MEB IIc 15695.

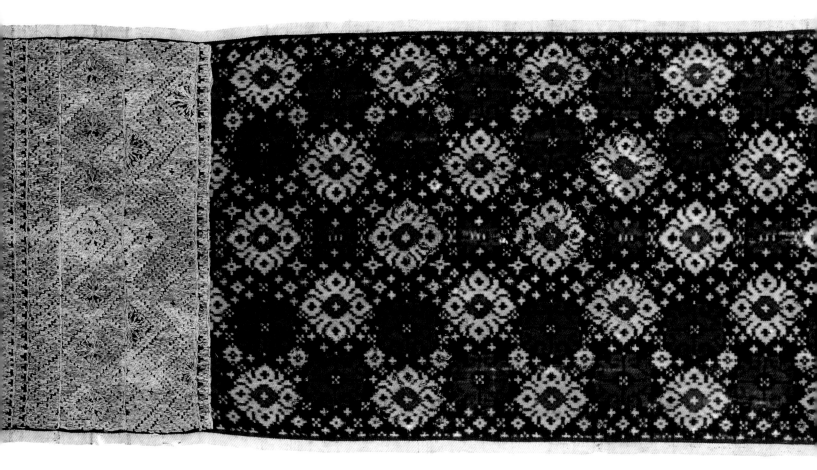

Figure 9.4: *Geringsing cemplong.* Tenganan Pegeringsingan, presumably early 20th century. 216 x 50 cm. MEB IIc 14150.

Studies of terminology have revealed an important criterion by which the local people distinguish *geringsing*. Generally speaking, the cloths are given the name of a fruit or a flower, and are often also referred to by pictorial terms whose meaning can no longer be elucidated. In certain cases, Balinese numbers are also appended to such expressions, so that for example one finds a *geringsing patelikur* (=24) *talidandan* or a *gering- sing cicempaka petang dasa* (=40). Further inquiries have indicated that these figures refer to different widths of cloth. Investigations have so far brought to light seven different widths, five of which are still made and worn in Tenganan today. A feature common to all these broad- width fabrics is that they are made up of a specific number of patterned warp strips, each consisting of 20 warp threads. Every strip contains a part of the whole design and all of them together produce the overall design of the cloth.

The narrowest cloths vary greatly in length, but are invariably composed of 14 patterned warp strips. Checked cloths of this type, the fringes of which are uncut, are worn by boys and men as tubular sashes (*sabuk tubuhan*) and knotted at the front of the chest or at loin height, so that the longer of the two ends formed by the knot hangs downwards. In the method of wearing known as *metangkon*, a particularly long cloth is worn in the same manner. In this case, however, the longer of the two ends is drawn over the head and placed around the neck (Fig. 9.10). Cloths of the same type with a cut fringe and decorated with floral or geometric motifs are worn by women and girls as breast cloths (*anteng*).

The cloths with 24 patterned warp strips and a cut fringe, similarly deco- rated with floral and decorative motifs, can also be worn by women and girls as breast cloths. However, it is more usual for two widths of woven

cloth to be sewn together along their length. In this form, they are worn by women as a top breast cloth, one end of the lower width of which is wrapped around so that it hangs down low over the buttocks (*makelukuh*). Men wear these cloths as an outer hip cloth (*saput*) over a hip cloth of normal length (*kamben batik* or *endek*). The cloths containing 37 and 43 patterned warp strips, with a central field divided into semicircular segments by large stars, are worn by women folded as a breast cloth, or draped over the right shoulder. The cloths with 40 patterned warp strips form a final category. Two widths are sewn together and worn by women and girls, mainly as an outer garment over a hip cloth containing a yellow-red tartan pattern. A third of the upper cloth width is turned down so that the cloth is draped twice over the chest and back.

PROTECTION AND DISTINCTION

As a microcosm of the universe created by the god Indra, the village of Tenganan Pegeringsingan is itself divine and omnipotent. The prime duty and principal aim of the village inhabitants is to play an active role in rituals honoring their gods, ancestors and demons. In this context, ritual clothing is a mandatory part of the divinely ordained scheme of things. In other words, the wearing of ceremonial apparel during communal and family rituals, and also on entering consecrated areas and buildings, is a divine injunction. Among the many fabrics from which ceremonial costumes may be composed, *kamben geringsing* take pride of place from the artistic, technological and religious points of view. As symbols of the divinely ordained exclusivity of this ritual community, such fabrics are both a mark of social identity while, at the same time, serving to preserve the purity on which the existence of the village and its inhabitants depends. Through their magical potency, they protect the

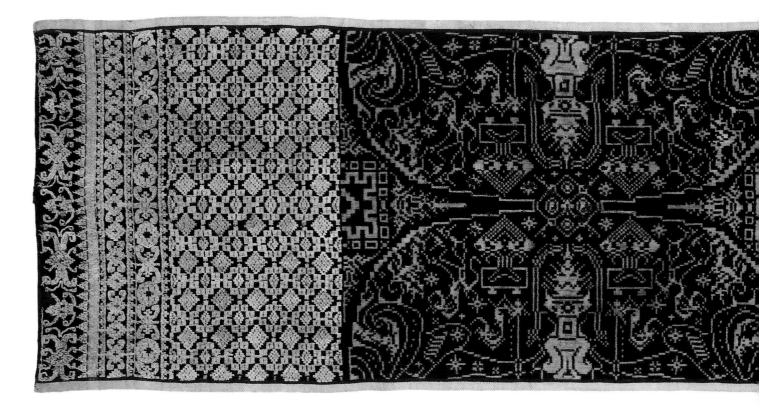

people of the community from the threat of defilement and decay.

In a special Tengananese version of the *Usana Bali*—a chronicle of a partly mythical and partly historical nature in which the creation, history and rituals of the Tengananese ancestors, the Wong Paneges, are described—it is written that when honoring the divinities many centuries ago, the high priest of the Balinese "mother temple" of Besakih, Sang Kulputih, wore multicolored cloths known as *rarajahan* with sun, dragon and mountain motifs. The villagers firmly believe that these were *geringsing* cloths, and since they conceive it to be their duty to maintain the heritage of their deified ancestors from Besakih, these special fabrics must form part of their own ritual wardrobe as well. Thus the village priest who is reputed to be the successor to Sang Kulputih, Mangku Désa, wears a *geringsing* with an uncut weft on his neck and hips while bidding the gods to descend and receiving them with all due honor. A divine injunction concerning such uncut cloths is reflected in the fact that they are also ritually offered to the gods as articles of apparel in *rantasan* or fabric offerings (Fig. 9.9).

Ritual clothing employing *kamben geringsing* is a mark of divine election to the community—incontestable evidence that the wearer belongs to the *désa adat* of Tenganan founded by Batara Indra. *Kamben geringsing* have thus become a kind of proprietary mark of Tenganan, a social emblem with which the members of this *désa adat* adorn themselves whenever they receive guests from the outside, or when they accept invitations from a friendly village and visit temples outside the village to participate in sacrificial rites and prayers.

The superlative aesthetic qualities of *kamben geringsing* have given it universal appeal. The wearing of the cloths enhances one's self-esteem and undoubtedly also possesses an inward efficacy, for they are usually worn on occasions of festive joy when it is fitting to adorn oneself for god and for one another. These include festive visits and receptions among the

Figure 9.5: *Geringsing isi.* Tenganan Pegeringsingan, presumably early 20th century. 218 x 53 cm. MEB IIc 17010.

various village organizations, and splendid rites of passage which constitute special celebratory occasions within the family circle. Formal exchanges—of services, gifts of the most diverse kinds, banquets, dances and musical performances—all form part of the major ritual cycles of Tenganan.

The socio-ritual organizations of the village—the village council (*krama désa*), the three unmarried men's associations (*teruna*) and the three girls' associations (*daha*)—are all involved in a constant cycle of ritual giving and receiving. Their members highlight the importance attached to these transactions by dressing festively for the visits. Their apparel includes various kinds of *kamben geringsing* worn by the ritual groups which, together with other mandatory cloths, are combined to make various "uniforms" (*pepatuhan*).

Geringsing cloths with patterned fields formed by 14 or 24 patterned warp strips and a cut fringe are worn by girls and women as a breast cloth wound around the upper body. These may be combined with double *ikats* of a greater width, or two pieces sewn together, or can be teamed up with checked yellow-red *kamben désa* or black-white *saput gotia* to form a variety of costumes. In the solemn *abuang luh* dance, one longer part of the usual floral-pattern breast cloth (*geringsing cicempaka* or *cemplong*) (Figs. 9.3, 9.4) is drawn over the upper garment so that it hangs down as a loose end (*lamak*) in front of the body. *Abuang luh* is a meditative dance in which the girls (in the third, fifth and eighth months of the Tengananese calendar) and the women (in the fifth month) appear in festive array before the longhouses of the unmarried men. They then dance individually, eyes lowered and arms raised and swinging to the strains of three *selonding* ensembles.

The women and girls wear particularly costly apparel during celebrations of the fifth month, when all cult groups visit one another to convey formal invitations to joint rituals, give banquets, exchange ritual gifts and

dance. On these occasions, broader widths of *geringsing*, as a rule two widths each consisting of 24 or 40 patterned warp strips sewn together (*cicempaka* and *lubèng* are especially popular), are worn as an outer garment over a yellow-red checked *celagi manis* hip cloth.

The famous *geringsing wayang* cloths, whose central panel is decorated across the width of the cloth with anthropomorphic figures from the world of Hindu-Javanese myth, are usually offered as elements of sacrificial clothing for the divinities (*rantasan*) (Fig. 9.9). These must be immaculate, as yet unused by human beings, and their warp must be circular and uncut. Fabrics with a cut fringe are sometimes worn by women and especially by girls, mainly at predominantly social fêtes attended by the public. Thus, in one of their *rejang* dances during the first month, the unmarried girls all wear the famous *wayang kebo*. Finally, in the fifth month, duels (*karé*) fought by youths from the village and the surrounding area with shields and prickly pandanus leaves to exact a blood toll (*tabuh rah*) present the girls of wealthy families with an opportunity to flaunt their position and possessions before a wider public. This occasion calls for the display of a splendid family heirloom textile—a *geringsing wayang kebo* or a *wayang puteri*, completely undamaged if possible. It is draped around the shoulders as a status symbol that proclaims to the outside world one's membership in an exclusive village community, while at the same time also conveying subtle social distinctions to knowledgeable observers within the village.

The protective or defensive function of the *kamben geringsing* becomes clearly apparent on comparing the youths' and men's rituals, which as a rule involve receptions and exchange transactions of the kind already described. For these rituals, long and narrow *geringsing* fabrics are wound around the body like a sash (*metangkon*), which is knotted so as to make a narrow end and also a wider one that is drawn over the head and draped around the neck. In almost all cases this method of wearing the cloths is typical of purificatory, exorcistic or martial rites involving the use of weapons. Obviously the point being made here is that *geringsing* possess the magical power to ward off the harm wrought by natural and supernatural enemies, and to confer invulnerability on a bearer of arms.

Thus, for example, the four male members of the village council who escort female council members to the festival of the swings in the fifth month all wear *geringsing* cloths and carry stout round shields of plaited rattan. During these days, the three associations of unmarried men (*teruna*) perform exorcistic perambulations around the village with their iron gamelan instruments (*selonding*), and frequently meet in mock battles. The three *teruna* are distinguished from one another by their "uniforms" (*pepatuhan*) (Fig. 9.10). Members of the uphill meeting house wear a red jacket and a red gold-threaded hip cloth, with a ring of gold foil or of palmyra leaf forming the headdress. The members of the central longhouse wear a white jacket and a hip cloth dyed indigo blue and interwoven with gold threads or white cotton yarn. The *teruna* members

Figure 9.6: The children of Tenganan Pegeringsingan are given their first *geringsing* cloths at the age of five or six years during a hair-cutting ritual.

Figure 9.7 (opposite): In the swinging ritual of Tenganan Pegeringsingan the members of the girls' associations wear an overgarment of *geringsing* cloths made from two woven widths joined together.

from the seaward longhouse wear a white jacket with a white hip cloth and—as with the two other associations—a *geringsing* sash around the hips and neck.

The same apparel is worn while performing various exorcistic dances in which demons are personified and stab each other in symbolic mock battles fought with bundles of prickly pandanus leaves. The protective, or rather defensive function of the *geringsing* cloths, especially the sash the men wear around the neck and hips, becomes particularly apparent in the seventh ritual month, when one of the two masters of ceremonies (*tamping takon*) marches through the village, followed by the women councilors, scaring away demons and spirits with a long lance. Meanwhile the other master, wearing a *kamben geringsing* as well, sacrifices a bull in the chthonic temple (*pura dalem*).

RITES OF PASSAGE

By virtue of their magical qualities, *kamben geringsing* are not only capable of keeping impurities and danger out of the village, but also actively shield a human being from threats and baleful influences during rites of passage, when a person undergoes a critical transition from one phase of life to the next. During such rites, the costumes worn highlight the persons and situations as being exceptional and, besides offering protection, they also mark ritual acts by which an individual crosses certain social boundaries. Given the abundance of rituals performed in Tenganan Pegeringsingan to mark the stations a mortal journeys through in life, it is useful to draw a distinction between those that are more or less confined to the family circle, and those that provide admission to village organizations. A feature common to all of them is that they continually promote a human being's purity and eligibility to participate in rituals, enabling him or her, for example, to join the village council and take part in its rites—and finally, after death, to be united with Batara Indra, the god of creation.

In all the temples of Tenganan associated with family initiations, prayers are said for the succor and happiness of mother and child. The sacrificial gifts a father takes to the *pura jero* temple include a black and a red double *ikat* (*geringsing patelikur isi* and *geringsing cicempaka* or *lubèng*, respectively). The Tengananese receive their first *geringsing* article of clothing around the age of four to six years, in the context of a hair-cutting ritual known as *ngetus jambot* (Fig. 9.6). Members of the girls' association then cut the child's hair with an ancient pair of sacred shears. While this is taking place, the candidate stands in front of the house compound on a stone slab inserted in the ground, on which the powers of the underworld are propitiated with sacrificial offerings. The cut hair is placed in a plaited basket on a *geringsing* cloth that has been folded double. Then, in the pavilion on the house compound (*balé tengah*) in which the Tengananese enters and leaves the world, he is arrayed in his first *geringsing* cloth and taken to a sacred bath in the north for purification.

On the evening of the wedding ceremony, the bridegroom invites his in-laws to visit in his own parents' home. The newlyweds sit in the inner room of the house (*umah meten*) dressed in festal *geringsing* clothing. The couple's parents then enter the room in succession and greet the betrothed with symbolic gifts laid on a *geringsing* cloth: rolled betel leaves, Chinese coins with holes in the center, and a strand of white cotton yarn

Figure 9.9: Clothes sacrifice *saparadeg*. The divinity's garments consist of a black-white checked *gotia* cloth, a *geringsing patelikur isi* and a *keris* dagger. Tenganan Pegeringsingan.

Figure 9.8 (opposite): Members of a girls' association from Tenganan Pegeringsingan, dressed in *geringsing* fabrics, dance the ritual *rejang* dance.

symbolizing newly-established family bonds that will never be severed.

On their admission to the youth association, a boy or girl is carried in a *geringsing* cloth on his or her father's right shoulder to the meeting house. In the solemn closing ceremony of the *teruna nyoman* (initiation cycle) following a year of seclusion, the candidates wear *geringsing* cloths and *keris* daggers with gilded handles.

After death, the genitals of the deceased are covered with a hip sash of *geringsing*. Such cloths may not be used again in rituals and are therefore sold in the numerous art shops of the village. Finally, during the purification of the soul ceremony (*muhun*), the dead person, whose presence is symbolized by an inscribed palm leaf, is once more arrayed in a *geringsing* cloth (Fig. 9.14).

Many other examples could be cited of the ritual use of these double *ikat* fabrics in Tenganan Pegeringsingan. In most cases the cloths are kept in the house compound as family heirlooms. The village council itself has a number of unworn specimens with an uncut fringe that are lent to families or individuals for sacrificial purposes. *Kamben geringsing* also find their way to the outside world by gift or sale, and are especially esteemed because of their magical powers.

In numerous villages of east Bali (Bugbug, Bebandem, Asak, Padangkerta or Banjar Timbrah in Paksebali, which is near Klungkung and originally belonged to east Bali), for example, the fabrics are draped around divine seats or around portable shrines that are ceremonially carried to the sea, to a sacred spring, or to the great festival and subsequent "war of the gods" waged annually on Gumang Hill near Bugbug (Fig. 9.12).

Geringsing cloths are also used throughout Bali during various rites of passage to protect the celebrants and to mark a separation of sacred from profane areas. Those who can afford to do so wrap a *geringsing wayang* around the pillow on which the novice's head rests during tooth-filing ceremonies (Fig. 9.11). It follows naturally enough that magical *geringsing* cloths which have the power to ward off danger are also used to

Figure 9.10: The protective function of *geringsing* cloths and their power to ward off evil influences come clearly to the fore in ritual battles and exorcistical rites performed by youths and men.

cover corpses, or as a canopy over the tower in which the corpse is carried to the cremation ground.

Narrow cloths called *geringsing sanan empeg* are worn for 42 days by men after a younger and an elder brother have died. Such people, who are called *sanan empeg* ("broken yoke"), are said to be particularly efficacious in driving away rice pests during their period of ritual impurity. In Tenganan itself, however, this custom is not commonly observed.

RULES AND RESTRAINTS

Although ritual constraints or prescriptions might be expected in view of the divine origin and magical significance of *geringsing*, only a few are actually observed in the making of the cloths. None of the oldest inhabitants of the village can recall the strict rituals for dyeing and weaving variously mentioned in the Western literature. Attention must be paid to a few rules that cannot be explained in terms of technical requirements, but are mandatory for the protection and purity of the work on the grounds of religious belief, and therefore indispensable for its success.

As a general rule, no work should be done during menstruation. Further, during the production process, ritually prescribed periods have now and then to be observed. For instance, immediately after the process has been started, yarns soaked in candlenut oil (*Aleurites moluccana*, Balinese *tingkih*) and wood-ash water have to be stored for 42 days in an earthenware jar covered with a checked black-white cloth (*gotia*) for protection against spirits. The strands are then hung up to dry for 42 days and covered with open hibiscus blossoms as protection against witches (*léyak*).

The *ikat* process involves certain rules and restraints only in the case of *geringsing wayang*. Immediately after the first bindings have been tied, a small purification sacrifice has to be made consisting of blossoms, rolled betel leaves and lime, and two sets of eleven coins with holes in the center (*képéng*) strung on cotton yarn are tied to the two posts of the ikating frame. The last of the bindings (reserve patterns) on these cloths may only be tied by women who are past menopause.

Figure 9.11: Tooth filing in a *ksatria* family. The young women rest their heads on a *geringsing wayang*, which exudes a protective force to ward off dangers. Gianyar, Blabatuh.

Figure 9.12: Sedan chairs for the gods from the east Balinese village of Bugbug. They are effectively protected with *geringsing* cloths from Tenganan Pegeringsingan, which keep all harmful influences at bay.

Figure 9.13 (opposite): *Geringsing batun tuung*. Tenganan Pegeringsingan, 19th or early 20th century. 258 x 40.5 cm. MEB IIc 14125.

HISTORICAL BACKGROUND

Kamben geringsing are of great importance for all Balinese, irrespective of whether they are used for black or white magic. It is hardly surprising, then, that even the rulers of early kingdoms in East Java sought to avail themselves of the services of Tengananese textile specialists whose mysterious cloths were employed to maintain and augment their power. Close study of the iconography of the *geringsing wayang* reveals striking comparisons with East Javanese temple reliefs of the 13th and 14th centuries. Especially the reliefs of Candi Jahagu (near Singosari), Candi Penataran (near Blitar) and Candi Tigawangi (near Paré) show amazing similarities with the representations of priests and heroes on *geringsing wayang kebo* and *wayang putri*. Other fabrics show patterns which are reminiscent of western Indian *patola* textiles, which also enjoyed great popularity in Hindu-Javanese court circles at this time.

It is particularly interesting to find the word *geringsing* mentioned in important literary works relating to the period when the aforementioned reliefs performed a didactic function. In Canto 18 of the *Nagarakrtagama*, an ode composed in 1365 by the Buddhist sage Prapañca in honor of the king of Majapahit, the poet describes with his customary thoroughness the composition of the royal caravan. It comprised six groups, distinguished by various emblems. The curtains of the carriage bearing the king, Hayam Wuruk, consisted of *geringsing, lobheng-lewih, laka*, etc., with ornaments.

The well-known *Pararaton* chronicle and a poem called *Rangga Lawé* (two East Javanese texts telling of the first king of Majapahit, Wijaya)

Figure 9.14: Purification of the soul in Tenganan Pegeringsingan. A young coconut-palm leaf inscribed with the name of the dead man and draped with his clothes serves as an effigy.

both relate that the king gave his warriors *geringsing* clothing prior to battle. In the *Pararaton,* five soldiers are given trousers of *geringsing* materials; in the *Rangga Lawé* all the warriors are provided with sashes called *cawet geringsing.* The magical potency of the double *ikat* of Tenganan clearly seems to have worked beyond the borders of Bali at a very early date, which is hardly surprising in view of the close cultural ties that existed between Bali and East Java in the early 10th century, and of the colonization of Bali by Majapahit after 1343. *Geringsing lubèng,* with its powerful star pattern on a bright red background, was particularly esteemed as the emblem and wardrobe of kings. Still today, this pattern is held to possess the highest prestige in Tenganan. Its aesthetic attraction and power has recently gained a reputation all over Bali. *Endek* cloth with *geringsing* patterns have become a real fashion hit (Fig. 2.13).

The identity and origin of figures represented in the *geringsing wayang kebo* and *wayang puteri,* which so clearly reflect the East Javanese style, pose questions of great interest for the cultural historian. One possible answer is that these fabrics, which are seldom worn in Tenganan, were originally designed and produced as commissioned works to meet the religious needs of the East Javanese and Javano-Balinese courts. The form and content of the *wayang kulit* (shadow play) are not known in the native village culture of Tenganan. On the other hand, the most popular of all Javano-Balinese kings, Dalem Batu Renggong, is reported to have clothed himself in *geringsing wayang* for his coronation.

Outside Tenganan, fabrics of the *wayang* type are still preferred today for use in the rites of passage celebrated by noble families, for example as a cloth in which to wrap the pillow during a tooth filing, or as a shroud to cover the body of the deceased before cremation. In many regions of Bali and among the Balinese of Lombok, *geringsing wayang* are suspended as a ceiling beneath the highest roof of towers used for transportation of a corpse. Fragments of magical *geringsing* cloth are also hung on sacred weapons or spread as an underlay for offerings, in the same way as *wangsul/gedogan.* In many old Balinese villages of east Bali, as well as in the famous temple of Samuantiga near Bédulu, the sedan chairs of the gods are swathed in *geringsing wayang.* When men perform the old *baris* war dances at temple festivals or death rituals (Badung, Tabanan, Bulèlèng), their wardrobe is often completed with the aggressive and at the same time defensive double *ikat* cloth from Tenganan.

Various myths, legends and historical documents suggest that the creators of *kamben geringsing* have not occupied their present site from "time immemorial." On the contrary, the story generally goes that ancestors of the Tengan. — the Wong Paneges or inhabitants of the original Balinese village created by the god Indra—came here in the distant past from the kingdom of Bédahulu in east Bali in search of a royal horse that had escaped. Royal edicts from the 11th century show that, at this time, the settlement of "Tranganan" was still located on the coast at Candi Dasa, and that the inhabitants had close links with the famous Javanese ambassador and religious reformer Empu Kuturan, who lived only a few kilometers away in Silayukti (near modern-day Padangbai). In an important *lontar* (palm leaf) historical text preserved in the Jero Gedé of Sidemen, the *Babad Bali Pulina,* there is also an account of close relations between the Bali Aga of "Tranganan" and Kuturan. At the same time, the reader of this chronicle finds the intriguing statement that a sect dedicated to Indra landed on the coast at Candi Dasa following a shipwreck.

In point of fact, relics carried even now in a procession from the *balé agung* of Tenganan to the Sembangan temple in the northern part of the village, are said to be fragments of the raft that brought the ancestors of Tenganan across the sea and broke up and sank shortly before landing. A sea-mindedness, which clearly distinguishes the Tengananese from the mountain-mindedness of the other Balinese, is suggested by two other cultural elements. The original altar (*sanggah kamulan*) of all house compounds in Tenganan is oriented in the direction of the sea and not towards the volcanoes and the sunrise (*kaja-kangin*), as in other Balinese villages. Secondly, the people of Tenganan do not practice cremation. Once the sun is past its zenith, the body is carried to the cemetery, where it is undressed and placed naked in the grave, the head face down, pointing in the direction of the sea.

Genetic and medical research begun in 1978 by a team of Indonesian and Swiss scientists in Tenganan Pegeringsingan has even suggested the possibility that the people of Tenganan originally came to Bali from India, either direct by sea, or via Java. Tests have revealed that 18 inhabitants of the village have in their blood a special enzyme, L H D Calcutta 1, which is characteristic of Indians and otherwise exceptionally rare outside India. The supposition that Indra's sect might be Vedic emigrants from India is bolstered by ethnographic findings. The most important ritual month of Tenganan coincides with the winter solstice. The complex swinging ritual that takes place at this time (Fig. 9.7) is strongly reminiscent of ancient Vedic swinging rites, which also take place at the time of the solstice (*mahavrata*) and are devoted to the god Indra, linking together heaven and earth. Moreover, our own surveys of textile technology in connection with double *ikat* do not, a priori, rule out an Indian origin, especially from Andhra or Orissa.

—*U. Ramseyer*

Figure 9.15 (opposite): Detail from a *Geringsing wayang* (no more specific designation is known). Tenganan Pegeringsingan, presumably 19th century. The iconography shows definite links with East Javanese designs of the 13/14th century. 229 x 56 cm. MEB IIc 17786.

Glossary

anteng	breast cloth for women
ATBM	*alat tenun bukan mesin* ("unmechanized loom"), a treadle loom with flying shuttle
atu-atu	ceremonial cloth with continuous warp, blue-white stripes, used for rites of passage
bagu	white ramie, *Boehmeria nivea* Gand
banji	pattern with meander pattern and T-forms
bebali	ceremonial cloths for gods and men
benang Bali	"Balinese thread"; handspun yarn of locally-grown cotton used for ritual purposes
cagcag	Balinese backstrap tension loom with yoke, reed, lease bar and heddle rod (see Chapter 3)
cepuk	special type of weft *ikat* cloth (see Chapter 8)
cerik	shoulder breast cloth for women
destar (HB)	men's headcloth
endek	weft *ikat*
galeng tumpuk	cylindrical cushions of *bebali* cloths piled one on the other, at tooth filing rituals
gedogan	ceremonial cloths with continuous, circular warp
geringsing	double *ikat* cloths from Tenganan Pegeringsingan
gigi barong	"Barong's teeth"; a pattern consisting of bands of white triangles on the edges of *cepuk* cloths
ikat	resist technique in which the yarn is tie-dyed before weaving (see Chapter 2)
kamben (LB)	inner hip cloth for men, hip cloth for women
kampuh (HB)	outer hip cloth for men
kapas	cotton
kebaya	a Javanese-style blouse, now considered part of the Indonesian national costume; forms part of the ceremonial dress in Bali
keling	striped or checked cotton material from Nusa Penida (see Chapter 6)
kemiri	candlenuts, *Aleurites mollucana*
kulangsih	*bebali* hip cloth, checked black and white

kunyit	turmeric, *Curcuma domestica*
kupas	young banana bast, used for tying in the *ikat* process
lamak	ornamental hanging of palm leaves or cloth
nuduk	setting up of pattern heddle rods (see Chapter 3)
nyatri	application of dye to bundles of yarn in making *endek* and *cepuk*
pakekek (HB)	women's sash or band
patola	silk double *ikat* cloth from Gujarat (India)
penganyinan	warping device
perada	patterning technique using gold leaf, gold dust, bronze pigment paint, or gold plastic foil
perémbon	*wangsul* or *bebali* cloth with stripes, used in rites of passage
polèng	black-and-white checked cloth
raina-wengi	literally: "day and night;" ceremonial cloths in black and white, used in votive offerings
rantasan	pile of cloths, as part of votive offering (also called *tigasan*)
sabuk (LB)	sash
saput (LB)	outer hip cloth for men
sekordi	*bebali* cloth in red, yellow, black or green; worn as a hip cloth in rites of passage
seléndang	breast or shoulder cloth for women
selulut	*bebali* cloth with check pattern, used in tooth filing rituals
sinjang (HB)	inner hip cloth for women
songkèt	cloth with continuous or discontinuous supplementary wefts of metal threads
suddhamala	"free from harmful influences"; cloths that confer protection
sunti	*Morinda citrifolia*
tapih (LB)	inner hip cloth for women
taum	indigo
tulad	sample as guide in *songkèt* weaving
udeng (LB)	men's headcloth
ules galeng	sacred covering of the pillow during tooth filing
usap rai	*wangsul* cloths with depictions of the love gods Semara and Ratih, used in *mapedamel* ceremonies
wangsul	ceremonial cloth with continuous, circular weft
wastra (HB)	inner hip cloth for men, hip cloth for women

Bibliography

GENERAL LITERATURE

Bali, Studies in Life, Thought, and Ritual. Foris. Dordrecht 1984 (1960).

Bali, Further Studies in Life, Thought, and Ritual. W. van Hoeve. The Hague 1969.

Belo, J. (ed.): *Traditional Balinese Culture*. New York, London 1970.

Berg, C. C.: *De middeljavaansche historische traditie*. Santpoort 1927.

Covarrubias, M.: *Island of Bali*. London, Toronto, Melbourne and Sydney 1937.

Goris, R.: *Bali. Atlas Kebudajaan. Cults and Customs*. Jakarta 1953.

Goris, R.: *Prasasti Bali*. 2 vols. Bandung 1954.

Hanna, W. A.: *Bali Profile. People, Events, Circumstances (1001-1976)*. New York 1976.

Hooykaas, C.: *Religion in Bali*. Iconography of Religions, XIII/10. Leiden 1973.

Hooykaas, C.: *Cosmogony and Creation in Balinese Tradition*. The Hague 1974.

Korn, V. E.: *De dorpsrepubliek Tnganan Pagringsingan*. Santpoort 1933.

Mershon, K. E.: *Seven Plus Seven. Mysterious Life-Rituals in Bali*. New York 1971.

Pigeaud, T. G. T.: *Java in the 14th century: a study in cultural history*. The Hague 1960-63.

Ramseyer, U.: *Bali. Insel der Götter*. Ausstellungsführer des Museums für Völkerkunde Basel. Basel 1983.

Ramseyer, U.: "Désa Adat Tenganan Pegeringsingan. Sozio-rituelle Organisationen einer altbalinesischen Kulturgemeinschaft" in: W. Marschall (ed.): *Der grosse Archipel. Schweizer Ethnologische Forschungen in Indonesien. Ethnologica Helvetica 10*, 1985: 251-273.

Ramseyer, U.: *The Art and Culture of Bali*. Singapore, Oxford, New York 1986.

Van der Tuuk, H. N.: *Kawi-Balineesch-Nederlandsch Woordenboek*. 4 vols. Batavia 1897-1912.

TEXTILES

Bolland, R.: "A Comparison between the Looms used in Bali and Lombok for Weaving Sacred Cloth" in: *Tropical Man IV*, 1971 171-182.

Bühler, A.: "Materialien zur Kenntnis der Ikattechnik." *Internationales Archiv für Ethnographie, Supplement XLIII*, 1943.

Bühler, A.: "Patola influences in Southeast Asia" in: *Journal of Indian Textile History IV*: 4-46.

Bühler, A. and E. Fischer: *The Patola of Gujarat*. Basel 1979.

Bühler, A., U. Ramseyer and N. Ramseyer-Gygi: *Patola und Geringsing: Zeremonialtücher aus Indien und Indonesien*. Ausstellungsführer Museum für Völkerkunde Basel 1975.

Damsté, H.T.: "Balische kleedjes en doeken, verband houdende met eeredienst en doodenzorg" in: *Koninklijk Instituut voor de Taal-, Land- en Volkenkunde van Nederlandsch Indië. Gedenkschrift uitgegeven ter gelegenheid van het 75-jarig bestaan op 4 juni 1926*. 'S-Gravenhage 1926: 254-264.

Gittinger, M.: *Splendid Symbols*. Washington 1979.

Hauser-Schäublin, B.: "Der verhüllte Schrein. Sakralarchitektur und ihre Umhüllung in Bali" in: *Ethnologica Helvetica 16*. Bern. (in press).

Hooykaas, C.: "Patola and Geringsing: An Additional Note" in: *Bijdragen tot de Taal-, Land- en Volkenkunde 134 (2-3)*, 1978: 356-359.

Jasper, J.E. and Mas Pirngadie: *De Inlandsche Kunstnijverheid in Nederlandsch Indie, II: De Weefkunst*. 'S-Gravenhage 1912.

Khan Majlis, B.: *Indonesische Textilien. Wege zu Göttern und Ahnen*. Rautenstrauch-Joest-Museum für Völkerkunde. Köln 1984.

Langewis, L.: *A Woven Balinese Lamak*. Royal Tropical Institute No. CXIX, Amsterdam 1956.

Loebèr, J.R. Jr.: *Textiele Versieringen in Nederlandsch-Indië*. Amsterdam 1914.

Maxwell, R.: *Textiles of South-East Asia. Tradition, Trade and Transformation*. Melbourne, Oxford, Auckland, New York 1990.

Nabholz-Kartaschoff, M.L.: "Preliminary Approach to Cepuk Cloths from South Bali and Nusa Penida" in: *Indonesian Textiles—Summing up Findings and Problems. Symposium held within the Scope of the Research Project "Indonesian Textiles—Museum Collections in the State of North-Rhein-Westfalia."* Cologne (in press).

Nabholz-Kartaschoff, M.L.: "A Sacred Cloth of Rangda. Kamben Cepuk of Bali and Nusa Penida" in: M.Gittinger (ed.): *To Speak with Cloth. Studies in Indonesian Textiles*. Museum of Cultural History, Los Angeles 1989: 181-197.

Pelras, C.: "Tissages Balinais" in: *Objets et Mondes II*, l, 1962: 215-239.

Ramseyer, U.: "Double Ikat Ceremonial Cloths in Tenganan Pegeringsingan" in: *Indonesia Circle 30*, London 1983: 17-27.

Ramseyer, U.: "Clothing, Ritual and Society in Tenganan Pegeringsingan (Bali)" in: *Verhandlungen der Naturforschenden Gesellschaft Basel 95*, 1985 (1984): 191-241.

Ramseyer, U.: "The Traditional Textile Craft and Textile Workshops of Sidemen, Bali" in: *Indonesia Circle 42*, London 1987.

Ramseyer, U. and N. Ramseyer-Gygi: "Bali, Distrikt Karangasem. Doppelikat in Tenganan Pegeringsingan, I-IV" in: *Publikationen des Instituts für den Wissenschaftlichen Film Göttingen*. Series 9, Nos. 11-14. Göttingen 1979.

Warming, W. and M. Gaworski: *The World of Indonesian Textiles*. Tokyo/New York 1981.

Wirz, P.: "Die magischen Gewebe von Bali und Lombok" in: *Jahrbuch des Bernischen Historischen Museums 11*, 1931 (1932): 39-49.

Yoshimoto, S.: *Indonesia senshoku taikei* (Outline of Indonesian textiles). Vol. 1. Kyoto 1977.

Yoshimoto, S.: *Kain Perada. The Gold-Printed Textiles of Indonesia*. Kyoto 1988.

Index